C000164636

Critical Guides to French Texts

92 Molière: Le Bourgeois gentilhomme

Critical Guides to French Texts

EDITED BY ROGER LITTLE, WOLFGANG VAN EMDEN, AND
DAVID WILLIAMS

MOLIERE

Le Bourgeois gentilhomme

David Whitton

Senior Lecturer in French Studies
University of Lancaster

Grant & Cutler Ltd
1992

© Grant & Cutler Ltd 1992

ISBN 0 7293 0339 X

I.S.B.N. 84-599-3275-3
DEPÓSITO LEGAL: V. 750 - 1992

Printed in Spain by
Artes Gráficas Soler, S.A., Valencia
for
GRANT AND CUTLER LTD
55-57 GREAT MARLBOROUGH STREET, LONDON, W1V 2AY

Contents

Preface   7

1. Critical Issues   9

2. Context: Genre and Occasion   15

3. Structure   27

4. Action   40

5. Significance   66

Bibliography   78

Preface

What we call Molière's *Le Bourgeois gentilhomme* is a play which exists in its own right, as a text to be studied and as a script to be performed, with suitable accompaniments, as a theatrical work. For Molière's contemporaries, however, *Le Bourgeois gentilhomme* denoted something different, a multi-media *divertissement* of which the play was just one component, and probably not the most important one. The original *Bourgeois gentilhomme* was a collaborative creation, devised by Molière and the Court musician Lulli with the ballet-master Beauchamp and others. Although no record of the choreography has survived, other elements of the original entertainment have been preserved. One is the *Livre des intermèdes*, usually called the *livret*, which was distributed to spectators at the first Court performance. It summarises the action of the play and the various musical and danced *agréments* or *ornements*, as Molière called them. We are also fortunate to possess Lulli's music, transcribed by a later Superintendent of Royal Music, Philidor. These elements, together with Molière's text, constitute our principal records of the event which took place at the Château de Chambord on 14 October 1670.

This book is devoted primarily to a study of Molière's play as living theatre, rather than to a historical study of the Molière-Lulli *divertissement*. To some extent, of course, the distinction is impossible to maintain. The play's form and content were largely determined by the spectacle of which it was a part — or, as I prefer to think, of which it was the core. I shall, therefore, be making reference to the *livret* and to Lulli's score where these throw light on the conception or execution of the play.

It goes without saying that when reading a play some imaginative contribution is needed from the reader to form a mental image of what the play means in performance. What is true for conventional drama applies with special force to a musical spectacle such as *Le Bourgeois gentilhomme*. One of my aims in this study is to suggest how the play works in theatrical terms. Readers may also find it rewarding to listen to a recording of the play. The recording in the series 'L'Encyclopédie Sonore' (Hachette, ref. 320E 842-4) has a distinguished cast and includes a relatively full version of Lulli's music. However, it is a studio recording and somewhat lifeless as a result. I prefer the vastly superior dramatic and comic qualities of the live recording of Jean Meyer's production at the Comédie-Française (1955: Pathé, ref. DTX168-70; also on cassette: Clé International, 1988). Better still, there is the black-and-white film of the same production (1958). It is a valuable filmed record of a classic stage performance. A more recent film by Roger Coggio (1982) is, in contrast, a more adventurous but not entirely happy cinematic adaptation of the play. I find the attempt at realism inappropriate and the multiple locations distracting. Recordings of Lulli's music are of considerable interest in their own right, though of course none of them conveys the dramatic qualities of the *comédie-ballet*.

In this study quotations from the play are taken from the Despois & Mesnard edition of Molière's *Œuvres*. Modern *éditions scolaires* may show some minor variations in punctuation and stage directions.

References to *Le Bourgeois gentilhomme* are given in the form of act and scene (e.g. III, 10). References to verse plays include line numbers (e.g. I, 5, v.339). Italicised numerals in brackets refer to numbered items in the Bibliography, followed by a page reference where applicable.

Acknowledgements

I am indebted to Janet Clarke, Susan Taylor-Horrex and Hilary Whitton who gave their time to read the script and made many valuable suggestions.

1. Critical Issues

Le Bourgeois gentilhomme is rightly considered the most accomplished and brilliant example of an especially seductive theatrical genre, the *comédie-ballet*. Composed for a major Court entertainment at the Château de Chambord in the autumn of 1670, it was Molière's tenth *comédie-ballet*, though the only one to which Molière himself attached that description. His other musical plays were called, variously, *comédie mêlée de chants, comédie mêlée de musique et d'entrées de ballet* or simply *comédie*. What they have in common is a blend of comedy, music, song and dance, and the fact that they were written to entertain the King and the Court. They were thus composed essentially as *divertissements* — though, as I shall suggest, this did not necessarily condemn them to triviality nor preclude them from outlasting the fleeting occasion for which they were written. Some of Molière's *comédies-ballets* depict graceful pastoral fantasies or mythological subjects. *Le Bourgeois gentilhomme*, an altogether more robust and rumbustious work, belongs to a different line of development, closer in subject-matter to satirical plays like *Tartuffe* and *L'Avare*, with characters drawn from the contemporary social scene. This, perhaps, is one factor that lifts the play above convention and gives it the human and social interest that ensures its perennial appeal.

Critical opinion has long been divided on the status of Molière's musical comedies. On the one hand, few would deny *Le Bourgeois gentilhomme* its claim to be the unrivalled entertainment piece of the seventeenth century. On the other hand, there is a long tradition of treating the *comédies-ballets* as a secondary facet of Molière's art, entertaining but little more. Implicit in such a view is some comparison with his 'straight' comedies — comedies of manners and ideas such as *Tartuffe* and *Le Misanthrope* — which are often held to represent the summit of his artistic achievement. In its extreme form, this approach has led critics to question the legitimacy of a hybrid genre where comedy and dance intermingle. 'Les comédies-ballets sont un genre faux', declared Larroumet, 'où le génie d'un grand écrivain était mal à l'aise' (*28*, p.292). Alternatively, it is suggested that in accepting royal commissions for Court entertainments, Molière was demeaning himself and trivialising his art. Voltaire, in his commentary on *Monsieur de Pourceaugnac*, reported that 'Les gens de bon goût reprochèrent à l'auteur d'avilir trop souvent son génie à des ouvrages frivoles qui ne méritaient pas d'examen.' It is probably true that Court audiences tended to look for spectacle and light entertainment rather than intellectual stimulation (*26*, pp.40-47). *Le Bourgeois gentilhomme* certainly supplied the former. But I find no evidence to suggest that Molière's aim was limited to producing an innocuous *divertissement*. In its treatment of human and social themes the play suggests a writer who approached his subject with the critical intelligence that he reveals in his so-called comedies of ideas.

If the objection is not one of triviality, it is that the *comédies-ballets* are dramatically flawed. *Le Bourgeois gentilhomme* is said to be badly constructed. Nothing could be further from the truth. Close study of the play, to which detailed attention will be given in Chapters 3 and 4, reveals a meticulous composition in which nothing is haphazard and every last detail is integrated into a harmonious scheme. The idea that the play is badly constructed is probably based on a fundamental misunderstanding about the nature of comedy-ballet. In one edition of *Le Bourgeois gentilhomme* we are told that the dramatic comedy suffers at the hand of the ballet component. Molière, we read, 'had to devote time and energy to the addition of the ballets and the *intermèdes* for Court entertainment which would have been better devoted to the comedy itself', with the result, it is claimed, that 'the creation of a truly great comedy was thwarted by the King's request for a Court *divertissement*' (*5*, pp.xlix-xl). Such a negative approach seems to me unhelpful. It has its roots in a tradition, prevalent in much of the nineteenth century, and into the present century, to read and perform the play as a straight dramatic comedy — in other words, to treat the musical and balletic elements as mere embellishments. But *comédie-ballet* is a performance art in which every element makes an indispensable contribution to the whole. Any attempt to treat it as conventional drama is therefore bound to produce a distorted judgement. Ironically, Molière himself anticipated just such a fate and warned against it in the preface to one of his *comédies-ballets*:

> On sait bien que les comédies ne sont faites que pour être jouées, et je ne conseille de lire celle-ci qu'aux personnes qui ont des yeux pour découvrir, dans la lecture, tout le jeu du théâtre ... il serait à souhaiter que ces sortes d'ouvrages pussent toujours se montrer à vous avec les ornements qui les accompagnent chez le roi.
> ('Au lecteur', *L'Amour médecin*)

Fortunately that tradition has been reversed. Spectacle and music are now habitually restored to the play in performance. At the same time, the present century has seen a major revision of critical attitudes towards this formerly neglected facet of Molière's work. Pellisson's study of the *comédies-ballets* initiated their rehabilitation in 1914 (*47*). More recently articles by Gérard Defaux and Odette de Mourgues, to whom I am equally indebted, have shed light on the play's structure and thematic content (*37, 46*). In a more general way, studies of Molière by W.G. Moore, René Bray and W.D. Howarth, showing the artist confronting the practicalities of his stagecraft, have also helped to promote a better understanding of a genre whose key lies in performance.

Setting aside the objection that *comédie-ballet* is a flawed genre, there remains the question of the ultimate status of musical comedies. If no-one now disputes that laughter need not imply frivolity, there remains a lingering suspicion that a comedy which gives such a large place to spectacle, and where realism gives way to riotous fantasy, cannot quite be taken seriously. A present-day authority, W.D. Howarth, while unreservedly acknowledging *Le Bourgeois gentilhomme* as a masterpiece at its own level, nevertheless suggests that its preference for fantasy over realism allows one to conclude that 'perhaps *Le Bourgeois gentilhomme* belongs to a lower order of comedy than *Tartuffe*, *Le Misanthrope* or *Les Femmes savantes*' (*26*, p.222). Even such an enthusiastic advocate as Pellisson ultimately accedes to the same view. 'Sans doute', he writes, 'c'est dans *Tartuffe*, dans *Le Misanthrope* et quelques autres chefs-d'oeuvre classiques que se marquent les qualités les plus hautes et les plus rares de Molière; c'est là qu'il est sur les sommets' (*47*, p.ix). This is an understandable point of view, but it implies a hierarchical classification of the genres with which not everyone would agree. On the contrary, for Sainte-Beuve the real pinnacle of Molière's achievement is reached by following the development of his writing from the early farces, through the high comedies of his mid-career, to the full-blown poetic and comic fantasies of his later years (i.e. *Monsieur de Pourceaugnac*, *Le Bourgeois gentilhomme*, *Le Malade imaginaire*). Thus: 'De la farce franche et un peu grosse du début, on se sera élevé, en passant par le naïf, le sérieux, le profondément observé, jusqu'à la fantaisie du rire dans toute sa pompe et au gai sabbat le plus délirant' (*31*, p.35).

If fantasy is not an escape from reality, but reality transposed to a higher plane, then Sainte-Beuve is surely right to see the last *comédies-ballets* as the culmination of a particular comic vision. Molière's habitual comic formula is to postulate an irrational attitude embodied in a character, then to explore the consequences of that attitude in friction with the real world. In many of his plays the unreasonableness of the situation is held in check by a double constraint: the aesthetic criterion of *vraisemblance*, and the moral structure of comedy, dispensing retribution and reward, which implies some restoration of normality. In the last of his *comédies-ballets*, however, Molière throws off these constraints and allows the logic of the irrational to run its full course, to the point where fantasy envelops the characters and displaces everyday reality. It is permissible, at least, to think that in substituting *fête* for the cold light of reason, Molière is penetrating even more deeply into the simple but infinitely rich proposition to which all his comedies are dedicated: in the words of one of his own characters, 'Les hommes, la plupart, sont étrangement faits' (*Tartuffe*, I, 5, v.339).

Whether or not this makes *Le Bourgeois gentilhomme* more profoundly true as a study of mankind than a supposedly more realistic play such as *Tartuffe*, remains a matter for personal taste. What can be affirmed with some certainty, however, is that Molière himself gave no sign of taking his Court plays any less seriously than other works, or of attaching less significance to them. It is true that they were written to order. But so too, in a different sense, were all his plays. As a professional showman Molière also wrote to please the paying public, whose taste he regarded as the final arbiter of his work. It would be quite wrong, therefore, to regard the commissioned pieces as remunerative chores, or to imagine that Molière was forced to bend his talent to meet the royal edict. It would be more accurate to say that enlightened royal patronage gave him the resources to pursue a line of work whose creative challenge interested him greatly.

Not the least interesting feature of *Le Bourgeois gentilhomme* is the way it attempts to break the mould of conventional theatre. At different moments in the history of the stage, artists have dreamed of creating a perfomance art which would combine the human and social dimensions of theatre with the emotive power of music and the rhythmic spectacle of dance. To mention two obvious examples, opera and musical comedy represent attempts — neither of them, it must be admitted, wholly satisfactory — to unite theatre and music. Where comedy is concerned, it is worth recalling that the word itself (derived from *komos* and *ode*, meaning a revel-song) betrays the remote origins of theatre in revelries involving song and dance. Later, in the fifth century BC, the comic playwright Aristophanes blended choral passages and song with satire and farce. This may be what Molière was referring to when he wrote of his first *comédie-ballet* that 'on pourrait [en] chercher quelques autorités dans l'antiquité' ('Avertissment', *Les Fâcheux*). In more recent times, Wagner's music-dramas reflect a desire to create an integrated art form organised on a theatrical basis. Wagner's ultimate ambition was to create what he called a *Gesamtkunstwerk* or total art-work in which all the arts would be united. In France, at roughly the same time, the Symbolists experimented with a form of theatre in which poetry, music and painting were blended. Coming still closer to our own time, the German playwright-director Bertolt Brecht wrote musical plays with roots in theatre and cabaret. The best of these, *The Threepenny Opera* (1928), with its firm theatrical basis and separation of dialogue from song, stands comparison with *Le Bourgeois gentilhomme*.

Molière's exploration of comedy-ballet, I suggest, can be viewed as an attempt, within the context of seventeenth-century classical theatre, to create a total art form appealing to all the senses and whose cumulative effect exceeds the sum of the parts. It was not, even within the context of French classicism which tended towards a strict separation of the different genres, without precedent. But it was by far the most successful. The abiding problem for all attempts at 'total theatre' is one of maintaining a satisfactory balance between the constituent parts. This difficulty is most evident in opera, where the dramatic content is often weak and subordinated to musical motive. The relationship between spoken dialogue and sung text is also problematic. How does one pass from speech to song without creating an impression of artificiality and undermining or interrupting the dramatic action? Molière's solution to these problems — not achieved in all his *comédie-ballets*, but triumphantly accomplished in *Le Bourgeois gentilhomme* — was to integrate the music and dance in such a way that they were underpinned by a solid dramatic foundation, and arose naturally out of the dramatic situation. In other words (and this is what distinguishes it from Lulli's opera) it is a theatre enriched by complementary arts, rather than a branch of music illustrated by action. The result is a unique and outstandingly successful blend of spectacle, character comedy and social satire. My aim in the following pages is to explore how Molière uses drama, music and dance to create this theatrical *tour de force*.

2. Context: Genre and Occasion

> Il a le premier inventé la manière de
> mêler des scènes et des ballets dans
> les comédies, et il avait trouvé par là
> un nouveau secret de plaire. (*21*, p.4)

Genre

It is interesting that in an age which affected to mistrust originality
— or at least to prize it less than manner and style — Molière was
valued for his absolute originality. That originality had many facets.
To mention only two: as a playwright, Molière's creation of 'serious'
comedy is completely without precedent. By serious comedy I mean
comedy which is consistently funny, yet at the same time deals with
major topical and human questions. And secondly, as an actor-
manager, Molière created for himself and his fellow-actors a new
style of acting. In opposition to the rhetorical style of delivery
prevalent in the theatre of the day, and to the highly stylised performance of farce, he created a more detailed realistic style based on
observation of how people behave in real life. Contemporaries
remarked on this style with expressions such as 'naturel' or 'pris sur
le vif'. Jealous rivals and high-minded critics may have condemned
it as popularist and vulgar, but it was enormously popular with his
public. The success of his company in Paris undoubtedly owed as
much to the appeal of this novel style of performance, as to the
comic vision of the author. To these things must be added a third
claim to absolute originality in the invention of the new genre of
comédie-ballet. In the 'oraison funèbre' cited above, Donneau de
Visé rightly laid stress on this sometimes neglected facet of

Molière's originality, which he evoked with the felicitous phrase 'un nouveau secret de plaire'.

But what was *comédie-ballet*, and where did it come from? In one sense it is inseparable from a single creative genius. It was Molière himself who created the genre, and developed it in partnership with the Court musician Jean-Baptiste Lulli, and it effectively ceased to exist with his death. Its inspiration lies in Molière's own passion for music and dance as well as his own non-academic, non-literary idea of a theatre of action and spectacle. But, of course, no artist works in a vacuum, and no art is created out of nothing. Looked at from another point of view, *comédie-ballet* was a genre simply waiting to be discovered. The ingredients, comedy, music and dance, were already loosely associated, or at least juxtaposed, in entertainments of the period. It required only an artist of vision to weld them together in a coherent art form. Moreover, *comédie-ballet* was the product of a particular set of circumstances, created by the demands of the moment in a specific milieu. But since its generic origins lie in the *ballet de cour*, it is here that our discussion must begin.

Theatre-going and dancing were two of the great passions in Louis XIV's Court, but before Molière ballet and theatre evolved alongside each other as entirely separate arts. Until the later seventeenth century the name *ballet* was applied loosely to a wide variety of entertainments involving song and dance in various combinations. Whatever is understood by the term, however, it was emphatically not a dramatic genre. It would also be anachronistic to think of ballet in the seventeenth century as something presented on a stage for a passive audience as modern ballet is. It was, rather, a participatory activity, a ritualised display whose participants, in baroque fashion, were simultaneously both actors and spectators. Although the 1660s witnessed the development of professional ballet, particularly after the founding of the Académie Royale de Danse in 1661, dancing was still an essentially courtly and aristocratic accomplishment, attaining its most elaborate expression in the *ballet de cour*.

Dance had long been one of the major pleasures of the French Court, becoming a veritable mania in the early years of Louis XIV's reign. Any event from a royal birth to a military victory was automatically celebrated by a major entertainment, and it was inconceivable that any Court entertainment should be planned without a ballet for its climax. Nor was it only at Court that dancing was all the rage: any household with the least social aspiration would have a dance at the slightest excuse. Even the provincial social climbers whom Molière depicts in *Les Précieuses ridicules* (1659) have their little *bal*. The young King himself was largely responsible for the resurgence of interest in ballet. He was a keen and, by many accounts, remarkably talented and graceful dancer. The *ballet de cour* gave the King an opportunity to display his skills in a context whose refinement and splendour appropriately reflected the Sun King's magnificence. The political system of absolutism also favoured the development of such courtly entertainments. The nobility, deprived of real political power and prevented by their social status from engaging in work, trade, or any other productive activity, had the leisure to indulge in aristocratic social pastimes. Indeed, it is possible to see in Court ballet a perfect image of the privileged, decorous and impotent existence to which the aristocracy was reduced under the absolute monarchy.

In the *ballet de cour* the element of spectacle predominated, with costumes, choreographed movement, ingenious machine-driven scenery and other amazing technical effects all combining to impress and delight the eye. Often the ballet was just one component of a much larger programme which included feasting, fireworks and waterworks. The grandest of such *divertissements* at Versailles lasted several days. The ballet itself, which could last for anything up to ten hours, combined vocal and instrumental music, recitation, ceremonial processions and formal dances. It was built round a certain number of major choreographed items called *entrées*, each depicting a poetic or allegorical subject. By the 1660s the Court ballet had established a conventional pattern: an overture, leading to a succession of *entrées* punctuated by poetry and song, culminating in a *grand ballet*. One can see a distant but distinct echo of this pattern in *Le Bourgeois gentilhomme* with its four *intermèdes*

(corresponding to the *entrées*) and *Ballet des Nations* (corresponding
to the *grand ballet*).

Although a poet would be involved to supply a libretto, any
dramatic content would be minimal or non-existent. Rather than a
narrative structure or plot, it was the mythological or allegorical
motifs that connected the various parts of the spectacle. From an
artistic point of view the *ballet de cour* may be said to be superficial
and incoherent. But that is really beside the point, since Court ballet
never pretended to be an artistic phenomenon, despite the large
number of artists who were commissioned to work on it. Their role
was simply to supply specialist skills to enhance the entertainment.
No unified artistic vision controlled its creation; the operation was
masterminded by the nobleman or dignitary who supervised the
ballet (when he did not delegate it to a servant). As one writer of the
time put it, 'il [i.e. ballet] n'est tenu que de plaire aux yeux, de leur
fournir des objets agréables ... et de belles images' (*15*, p.210). Its
sole object, then, was entertainment, and its motive was a desire for
self-representation by the Court. It is against this unpromising background that Molière's venture into theatrical ballet must be
appreciated.

In 1661 Nicolas Fouquet, Louis XIV's finance minister,
planned to entertain the King and Court at his newly-reconstructed
chateau at Vaux-le-Vicomte. The festivities involved a programme
of unprecedented extravagance and splendour which set the pattern
for the King's entertainments at Versailles later in the decade. It was
natural that Molière, whose recent triumphs in Paris with *Les
Précieuses ridicules* and *L'Ecole des maris* had made him the most
talked-about new star, should be summoned to contribute. As a result
Molière found himself working alongside the royal ballet master
Beauchamp. The play he wrote, *Les Fâcheux*, was not especially
memorable in itself but it may be considered a landmark in the
development of French theatre, for it was to all intents and purposes
the first *comédie-ballet*.

Les Fâcheux involves the efforts of a lover trying to keep an
amorous rendezvous but constantly being detained by a succession
of bores. The situation (in which one can detect an embryonic

version of a later masterpiece, *Le Misanthrope*) is a vehicle for comedy of the kind at which Molière excelled: satirical sketches of character types observed in a contemporary social milieu and drawn with devastating accuracy. It was just such a formula, deployed in the context of a one-act farce, that had established Molière's comic reputation in 1659, with *Les Précieuses ridicules*. In *Les Fâcheux*, appropriately, the targets are society bores (the ostentatious theatre-goer, the huntsman, the gambler), minor nuisances of a kind which the Court audience would recognise as a common occupational hazard. What is remarkable and new, however, is that the same basic situation which provides the plot is also represented through the non-verbal medium of dance in the *entrées de ballet* which follow each of the acts. In these, the lover becomes embroiled in a further series of choreographed obstacles in the shape of a game of *boules*, a brigade of Swiss guards and so on.

According to Molière, this novel formula combining comedy with ballet within a dramatic framework was more the product of circumstance than artistic vision, an improvised solution to a practical problem. In the play's Preface he writes:

> Le dessein était de donner un ballet aussi; et comme il n'y avait qu'un petit nombre choisi de danseurs excellents, on fut contraint de séparer les entrées de ce ballet, et l'avis fut de les jeter dans les entr'actes de la comédie, afin que ces intervalles donnassent temps aux mêmes baladins de revenir sous d'autres habits.

In other words, a shortage of dancers dictated a need for something to occupy the stage during costume changes, and 'it was decided' (he does not say by whom) that Molière should write something to fill the gap. Such a brief, it should be remembered, was not unusual. The Court ballet was a collaborative enterprise, and the role of a poet was limited to composing the necessary *morceaux* to flesh out the ballet and separate its various *entrées*. Nor could anything more have been expected in the circumstances: Molière had been recruited to the production team at extremely short notice, two weeks before the date set for the entertainment. It is at once remarkable yet absolutely characteristic of him that, instead of merely supplying the requisite trifles, he sought to reconcile the requirements of the courtly entertainment with his own self-imposed artistic demands. He explains:

> pour ne point rompre aussi le fil de la pièce par ces manières d'intermèdes, on s'avisa de les coudre au sujet du mieux que l'on put, *et de ne faire qu'une seule chose du ballet et de la comédie.* (Preface, *Les Fâcheux*: my italics)

The matter-of-fact tone could blind us to the reality that what Molière is describing is something absolutely new: not a *ballet de cour* with intermittent verse, nor a play punctuated with danced *intermèdes*, but a hybrid spectacle in which comedy, music and dance unite to illustrate a single dramatic idea. At least, that was the principle. In practice, it can be argued that the fusion of elements in *Les Fâcheux* is not complete. Molière himself was the first to acknowledge, in his Preface, that the danced *intermèdes*, while they extend and complement the action, are not a fully integral part of it, as they would be in *Le Bourgeois gentilhomme*. But it was a pleasing mixture which certainly heralded an original art form, and whose potential evidently intrigued Molière:

> Quoi qu'il en soit, c'est un mélange qui est nouveau pour nos théâtres ... et comme tout le monde l'a trouvé agréable, il peut servir d'idée à d'autres choses qui pourraient être méditées avec plus de loisir. (ibid.)

By 'tout le monde', in this case, Molière can be taken to mean both *la cour* and *la ville*. A few days later Molière was summoned by the King to perform the new play *en visite* at Fontainebleau, but it also enjoyed a long run of forty-two consecutive performances in the playwright's Paris theatre. La Grange's register shows that it was a popular success — always a major consideration for a company which was heavily dependent on box-office receipts. Indeed, the fact

that a taste for music and spectacle was not confined to Court
audiences but was becoming increasingly popular with the theatre-
going public, thus creating a second lucrative outlet for the
comédies-ballets, must have weighed heavily in Molière's attitude
towards the new genre.

The most immediate impact of Fouquet's celebrations, however, was on the development of Court entertainments. Inspired by
the spectacle and sumptuous setting of Vaux, Louis XIV resolved to
create a new palace and gardens of unrivalled splendour, where
Court life would be transposed into perpetual *fête*. Pausing only to
dismiss Fouquet for embezzling the State to fund his high living, he
immediately set to work to realise this ambition. Versailles, which
underwent a major reconstruction between 1661 and 1664, became
the setting for *divertissements* of unparalleled extravagance and to
which Molière would be summoned to contribute with increasing
frequency.

From about 1664, therefore, comedy-ballet came to occupy an
increasingly important part of Molière's output. Versailles was
inaugurated in 1664 with 'Les Plaisirs de l'Ile Enchantée', a four-day
baroque celebration to which he contributed a spectacular musical
fantasy called *La Princesse d'Elide*. The following year his company
was adopted by the King and took the title of Troupe du Roi. The
first play he composed for the King in his new capacity was *L'Amour
médecin*, another *comédie-ballet* of sorts. Before that, in January
1664 at the Louvre, he had staged *Le Mariage forcé* in which Louis
XIV himself took a role. That play was also significant in marking
the first full collaboration between Molière and Lulli, who were to
work together on a further nine comedy-ballets. Of Molière's output
of fifteen plays between 1666 and 1672, no less than eleven were
comédies-ballets.

But to speak of *comédie-ballet* as if it were a single genre is
misleading. As an experimental artist, Molière was constantly
modifying the formula according to the demands of the moment and
in the light of earlier successes and failures. Certain principles,
however, remain constant, and they can be traced back to his earliest
experiments with the genre. One is the resolve to make of the

comedy-ballet an essentially *theatrical* work, i.e. one where music and spectacle are incorporated into theatre, not the other way round. In this concept, dance, music and song are to be considered as an expansion of the language of theatre. Here Molière's ideas were at variance with those of Lulli, who believed the future lay with opera. They were also at variance with those of the Court audiences, who almost certainly regarded the *comédie* as merely the pretext for the *ballet*. Not surprisingly, there is no evidence that Molière ever subscribed to this view. The other key principle is the notion of an artistic *fusion* — not a mere juxtaposition of elements, but one where ballet and song are naturally integrated in the play. Reflecting on his first such experiment, he admitted that the blend was far from perfect, that there were 'quelques endroits du ballet qui n'entrent pas dans la comédie aussi naturellement que d'autres' (ibid.). Nevertheless, there is a clearly stated intention to 'ne faire qu'une chose du ballet et de la comédie'. In Chapter 3 we shall see with what success these ideas are implemented in *Le Bourgeois gentilhomme*.

Occasion

By the mid-1660s Louis XIV had assembled a team of loyal and talented specialists well versed in providing the royal entertainments. Among them were Benserade, the official Court poet and librettist who supervised Court spectacles until he was succeeded by Molière, and Carlo Vigarani, an Italian designer and brilliant inventor of stage machines, the technical mastermind behind the royal celebrations. Beauchamp was the leading choreographer; it was he who was largely responsible for the eventual pre-eminence of French ballet throughout Europe. There was also, above all, the Florentine Jean-Baptiste Lulli, an extraordinarily talented and ambitious musician, dancer and producer who collaborated with Molière on many productions before eventually supplanting him in the King's favour and becoming the superintendent of Louis XIV's entertainments. Molière, who first came to the King's notice in 1661 and quickly became one of his favourites, played an increasingly prominent role in the Court entertainments during the 1660s. Following Benserade's retirement in 1670 he received the title of *divertisseur du roi*.

In September 1669 the company performed *Monsieur de Pourceaugnac*, another *comédie-ballet*, at the Château de Chambord near Blois, which at that time served as a hunting lodge for royal parties. The following autumn they were again required to perform there. The commission to write *Le Bourgeois gentilhomme* was probably issued early in the summer of 1670. The King himself suggested the play's subject, as he had done six months earlier for *Les Amants magnifiques*. The Chevalier d'Arvieux, in his Memoirs, records the circumstances thus:

> Le roi, ayant voulu faire un voyage à Chambord pour y
> prendre le divertissement de la chasse voulut donner à sa
> cour celui d'un ballet, et comme l'idée de Turcs, qu'on
> venait de voir à Paris, était encore toute récente, il crut
> qu'il serait bon de les faire paraître sur la scène. (7, vol.
> IV, pp.252-53)

It is possible, as Lancaster conjectures, that Molière was already working on what was to have been a character comedy in the familiar mould of *L'Avare* but involving a social climber (*10*, pp.724-25). This would then have provided the substance of Acts III and IV, adapted to accommodate the required *turquerie* and to form the framework of a *comédie-ballet*. If this is so, the blend is seamless. *Le Bourgeois gentilhomme* was written during the summer of 1670, a more leisurely period of composition than the overworked actor-manager usually enjoyed. It permitted him to compose a play of outstanding finish and structural perfection, though it has not always been recognised as such.

D'Arvieux, a specialist in Turkish affairs, joined the habitual team of Molière, Lulli and Beauchamp as consultant on oriental manners and dress. The designer was Carlo Vigarani. *Le Bourgeois gentilhomme* was presented in one of the large rooms adjoining the central open staircase in the château on 14 October, with three more performances the following week. A further Court performance was requested on 8 November, this time at Saint-Germain, before a scaled-down production of the play opened at the Palais-Royal theatre on 23 November.

A number of legends surround the play. One anecdote, to which D'Arvieux refers in the quotation above, concerns the official visit of Soliman Aga to Louis XIV in November 1669. It is said that the Ottoman emissary insulted his hosts by affecting to be unimpressed by the regal splendours of his reception in the French Court. According to one tradition, therefore, the chief minister Colbert proposed the play to ridicule Turkish customs and so avenge the insult to his master. But, as Lancaster points out (*10*, p.725), the revenge could hardly be effectual, since the Turks had left Paris ten months earlier. Nor, in fact, does the play satirise the pseudo-Turks: the joke is entirely at the expense of M. Jourdain. It would probably be closer to the truth to say simply that a topical fascination with Turkish manners, reinforcing an existing fashion for things exotic, lay behind the King's suggestion for a *turquerie*. The same vogue gave rise to a wave of oriental *récits*, plays and operas, from Mairet's *Le Grand et Dernier Solyman* (1639) to Racine's *Bajazet* (1672) and Lulli's own Turkish ballet (performed at Court in 1660, now lost).

It has been suggested that M. Jourdain was intended to be a satirical portrait of Colbert himself. It is true that Colbert, like M. Jourdain, was the son of a draper. And it is possible to detect similarities between Molière's would-be gentleman and the Finance Minister, a snobbish *parvenu*, anxious to forget his humble origins, susceptible to flattery, aspiring to sophistication yet infallibly behaving at Court with, in the words of the King himself, 'l'air d'un bourgeois de Paris' (*40*). Molière does seem on (rare) occasions to have based satirical portraits on specific individuals. Moreover, Louis XIV not only tolerated but positively appreciated satire of his courtiers, provided he himself was not in the firing line. However, for the Court entertainer to have attacked a Minister as powerful and close to the King as Colbert would seem extremely imprudent. Molière's contemporaries, in any event, do not appear to have remarked on the likeness. An early biographer of Molière, Grimarest, reports (or, more probably, surmises) that when *Le*

Bourgeois gentilhomme was performed in Paris, 'chaque bourgeois y croyait trouver son voisin peint au naturel' (*24*, p.82). It might be added that there is no shortage of contenders for the dubious distinction of having served as a model for M. Jourdain, amongst the more far-fetched being a wealthy draper of the rue aux Fers named Guillaume Jourdain (1557-1608) (*42*)! But it would be fruitless to pursue these speculations further. The type of *nouveau riche* represented by Jourdain is so universal that it is both futile and unnecessary to think of *Le Bourgeois gentilhomme* as a *pièce à clef*. Molière's stated position was to stress the general nature of comedy: 'Ces sortes de satire tombent directement sur les moeurs, et ne frappent les personnes que par réflexion' (*La Critique de l'Ecole des femmes*, scene vi).

On a different scale of unreliability is the oft-repeated tradition that *Le Bourgeois gentilhomme* was given a chilly reception at its first performance. Its origin — 'Jamais pièce n'a été plus malheureusement reçue que celle-ci' — is again Grimarest (*24*, p.81). His story is that the King received the play in stony silence, causing the Court to regard the event as a flop, until, after the second performance, he delivered a favourable verdict. This is probably best treated as a piece of fanciful embroidery. In any event, contemporaries of the play (of whom Grimarest is not one) speak uniformly of the *comédie-ballet* as an unqualified triumph.

There is something extraordinary in the fact that an ephemeral spectacle designed to amuse a restricted audience on a specific occasion should have gone on to become one of the favourite plays of the French comic repertoire. Its popularity with the general public is a measure of the theatrical skill and comic vision of a Court entertainer who contrived to imbue a commissioned piece with universal interest. But it also remains a perfect model of Court entertainment as it had developed under Louis XIV. At every level it bears the stamp of the occasion for which it was devised. On a material level, a lavishly expensive spectacle on this scale would have been unthinkable without royal support. At a deeper level, Court taste is reflected both in the exuberant but graceful tone of the comedy and in the social perspective whereby the oddities of the mercantile class

are viewed with bemused indulgence. Above all, of course, the
divertissement de cour was designed primarily to entertain. The
same may well be true of every one of Molière's comedies. After all,
one of his most famous and persuasive statements of dramatic
principle is the rhetorical question he poses in *La Critique de l'Ecole
des femmes*: 'Je voudrais bien savoir si la grande règle de toutes les
règles n'est pas de plaire'. Nevertheless, when *Le Bourgeois gentilhomme* is compared with Molière's dramatic comedies, there is a
readily discernible difference of emphasis. *Comédie-ballet* appeals
more strongly and immediately to a desire for escapism. This shows
not only in the use of music and dance to appeal to the senses, but
also in Molière's treatment of the dramatic action, where there is a
stronger tendency towards fantasy and a more relaxed approach to
dramatic logic. In the following chapters we shall see how this
general character is reflected in the play's structure and action.

3. Structure

Theoretically, the play is badly constructed. If analysis is restricted to the dramatic action, it does indeed show some striking irregularities. The play as it stands is in five acts. In that respect, at least, it seems to follow the standard pattern for a regular classical play. The appearance is totally misleading. For one thing, the acts are of greatly varying length. The first act and the last are exceptionally short, each little more than one tenth of the total. Act II is twice as long as Act I. And Act III, which alone constitutes well over a third of the play, is longer than the first two acts together. In a conventional play such inequalities would create an impression of structural imbalance and would be perceived as unsatisfactory.

Apart from these technical irregularities, the development of the action reveals further peculiarities. Acts I and II consist of a series of sketches which provide a brilliantly entertaining illustration of a situation, but they set no plot in motion. Most unusually, the characters involved in the first two acts, having played their part, promptly disappear with the exception of M. Jourdain himself. It is as if the whole of the first two acts were a lengthy curtain-raiser to the action proper. In Act III a new set of characters is introduced, the familiar characters of a domestic comedy. Even then, it is still some little time before we are drawn into the first of the play's plots, namely the intrigue involving Dorante and Dorimène. In this plot M. Jourdain is cast in the role of lover, believing himself to be courting the Marquise, when in reality he is being manipulated by Dorante who is wooing Dorimène at M. Jourdain's expense. We can now see a retrospective technical justification for the business in Acts I and II: M. Jourdain is completing his education and learning new accomplishments in order to impress Dorimène. But this intrigue, having dominated the third act, is not pursued to a resolution. It fizzles out — or rather, is stamped out — in IV, 2 with Mme Jourdain's sudden intrusion into the party.

That, though, is only one strand of the action. There is a second, semi-independent plot in the shape of another love intrigue involving M. Jourdain's daughter and her suitor Cléonte. This element, which subsequently comes to dominate the action and motivates the climactic Mamamouchi ceremony, erupts without warning with Cléonte's indignant entrance in III, 8.

As Jacques Schérer has observed, 'il y là matière à deux pièces distinctes qui, dans *Le Bourgeois gentilhomme*, se succèdent, plutôt qu'elles ne se combinent' (*35*, p.8). It is true, as Schérer notes, that a superficial link is established between the two actions when Dorante joins forces with Cléonte to fool M. Jourdain, but this is a formal rather than logically inevitable connection.

These irregularities have led many critics to conclude that the play has a weak dramatic structure. 'La pièce est bâtie à la diable', says Adam (*6*, p.383). For Bray, 'le ballet final était mal lié à l'ensemble' (*17*, p.260). Faulty construction is a charge often levelled against a great many of Molière's plays. In Molière's defence, it is usual to excuse so-called careless composition by pointing out either that he was often forced to compose very quickly (which is true) or that, in any case, such defects do nothing to detract from the spectator's enjoyment of the play. Adam, for example, writes: 'Ces défauts seraient graves si *Le Bourgeois gentilhomme* était une grande comédie. Ils n'ont aucune importance dans une *comédie-ballet*, et celle-ci ... est une des oeuvres les plus heureuses de Molière' (*6*, pp.383-84). Both these defences are valid, and we could leave the matter there, except that to do so would be to do a serious injustice to a craftsman of theatrical spectacles at the height of his powers. For Molière was essentially a man of the theatre. A critical approach which forces us to assume that his command of his craft was defective must surely be treated with some suspicion. To speak of defects (excusable or otherwise), almost certainly suggests that we have failed to penetrate the secret of the play's composition. It will be more fruitful to discard literary and academic ideas about plot, and enquire what structural principle Molière employed in writing *Le Bourgeois gentilhomme*.

As always, it is essential to remember that *comédie-ballet* is a performance art. In composing his play, Molière did so in the knowledge that it was destined to be one element in a larger entity of which ballet and song were integral parts. If we analyse this entity, *Le Bourgeois gentilhomme* reveals an extraordinarily tight and harmonious construction.

We must begin by disregarding the play's division into acts. They are a convention observed in the printed text but which have no real meaning in *Le Bourgeois gentilhomme*. Since the action runs continuously throughout the play, the spectator (as opposed to the reader) is unaware of the acts. What the spectator perceives is a single continuous action in which the various media — dialogue, dance, music and song — alternate and combine to create a unified theatrical experience.

Analysis of this total entity reveals not a dramatic structure in five acts but a musical structure in three movements of roughly similar proportions. These correspond to:
— Acts I and II
— Acts III and IV
— Act V and the Ballet des Nations
Each movement builds towards a climax, each more spectacular and fantastical than the previous one, and the entire structure is crowned by the final Ballet des Nations. The syntax which binds the different elements together and articulates them is not the syntax of drama (i.e. plot) but the syntax of music and dance — namely, rhythm and choreographed movement. As in a musical composition, there are echoes, contrapuntal movements and resolutions which give form and variety to the piece.

First movement

Acts I and II can be considered as two phases of a single movement. They are preceded by an overture, 'qui se fait par un grand assemblage d'instruments', and about which more will be said below. The play proper begins when the orchestra falls silent, leaving the Musician's pupil, on stage, composing a serenade. From then on, there is a steady amplification, as more characters are introduced to the stage, building by degrees towards the first major set-piece, the *bergerie* at the end of Act I. The action continues without interruption: 'Voilà qui n'est pas sot', says M. Jourdain at the end of the dance, giving a natural transition to dialogue again. The second phase of the movement, i.e. Act II, resembles a *reprise* of the first, though it is somewhat longer, as is appropriate, more sustained, and proceeds to a second *intermède*, more substantial than the first.

Looking at this movement more closely, we can see how Molière uses the different performance media to create structural patterns. The play is preluded by a musical motif (the serenade). This is subsequently picked up in the action when it is presented to M. Jourdain for his approval, and followed by a burlesque parody when M. Jourdain sings his preferred rustic song ('Je croyais Jeanneton...'). So far, the only *ornements* have been musical ones. The first phase culminates in the *intermède* where, for the first time, dance is combined with music. The *bergerie*, however, also initiates the second phase of the movement. From this point, quite appropriately therefore, dance takes over from music as the dominant *ornement*. Certain comic situations from the first phase are repeated or echoed in the second. M. Jourdain's first dancing lesson (II, 1) offers a parallel to his initiation to singing (I, 2). On this occasion the pupil's inept attempt at a minuet is set against the elegant movements of the master, echoing M. Jourdain's parody of the serenade in Act I. This is followed immediately by a minor echo of the same motif, with M. Jourdain learning how to bow, and then by a more substantial *reprise* with the fencing lesson (II, 2), itself a dance of sorts. The movement then builds towards the full balletic sequence of M. Jourdain's *habillement*, which also prepares for the tailors' *intermède*.

The whole movement, then, is built on a structural principal which is not a dramatic one but a musical one, involving echoes, complementary movements and contrasts. Molière skilfully introduces his different 'instruments' (first music, then song, then dialogue, then dance) in carefully phased stages. The Maître de Musique himself alludes to this cumulative effect when he tells M. Jourdain: 'Lorsque la danse sera mêlée avec la musique, cela fera plus d'effet encore' (II, 1).

The overall pattern — like that of the play as a whole — is based on a rhythm of progressive amplification. It starts with a solo (the musician's pupil), develops into a duet (the Maître de Musique and the Maître à Danser), and swells to a trio with the arrival of M. Jourdain. We note also that there are 'deux violons, trois musiciens, quatre danseurs'. The first song is, of course, the solo serenade, which develops into a musical duet of sorts with the exchange between the serenade and M. Jourdain's own song. The next song, the 'Dialogue en musique', is a tercet sung by 'une musicienne et deux musiciens', and is followed by a quadrille where 'quatre danseurs exécutent tous les mouvements différents'. More characters are then introduced — the Maître de Philosophie and the Maître d'Armes — producing a more crowded, animated and noisy action. The action then proceeds towards a boisterous first climax (the fight), subsides to a lengthy *scène à deux* of sublime ridicule (the philosophy lesson), then, with the appearance of the Maître Tailleur, builds again to the true climax of the movement, the burlesque ceremonial of M. Jourdain's *habillement*. The *livret* for the original performance, incidentally, shows that M. Jourdain is dressed by six 'garçons tailleurs', rather than the four mentioned in the printed text, underlining the mathematical progression of the characters (*1*, p.231).

Second movement

In musical terms, the second movement develops in greater amplitude the themes explored in the first. After the prelude, it is fuller and richer. As well as the central theme of obsession and gullibility, there are many visual cross-references to the earlier acts, with M. Jourdain ludicrously attempting to demonstrate his new accomplishments: fencing (III, 3), phonetics (ditto), bowing to a *marquise* (III, 16). As in the first movement, Molière's chief concern is to

develop the portrayal of his central character. In contrast with the
first movement, where the character was shown in a succession of
tableaux, we now see him in the context of a dynamic action. As
noted above, two plots are set in motion, the one figuring M. Jourdain as would-be lover, the other representing him as an unreason-
able *père de famille*. The two arenas of action are developed in
parallel, rather than in unison, before converging in the major
balletic set-piece of the Mamamouchi ceremony.

At first, though, the play seems to have switched to a different
mode, with a new set of characters involved in a domestic comedy.
And one might wonder what has become of the musical and balletic
accompaniments which featured so prominently in the first
movement but which appear to have been abandoned in favour of a
dramatic action conducted solely in dialogue. At the centre of the
play there is a long third act apparently devoid of spectacle until the
very end. In fact, the musical rhythm of the first movement has not
been discarded in the domestic comedy of Act III. Even before the
formal dances and songs are re-introduced, musical and balletic
motifs are woven into the dialogue. Act III scene 2, where M.
Jourdain, parading in his new outfit, is laughed at by Nicole, has a
musical structure of its own. Molière develops it in three phases. It
begins with an initial spontaneous outburst of laughter which stops
M. Jourdain in his tracks and which he only succeeds in suppressing
by threats ('Si tu ris encore...', etc.). This is followed by a phase
where M. Jourdain resumes his instructions, periodically interrupted
by the servant's muffled and only half-stifled laugh. Finally, the
laughter can be suppressed no longer, and explodes in unconstrained
hilarity, more helpless than before. This musical phrasing, which a
sensitive director or actress will discover on speaking the lines, is not
in the least arbitrary or accidental. A more obvious example, which
will be discussed further in chapter 4, is the lovers' quarrel in III, 9-
10. Here, a dialogue presented with the formal movements of a *pas
de deux* develops into a fully balletic quadrille.

As for the *ornements*, they are not forgotten but are being held
in suspension. The effect is all the greater when they are re-introduced. At the end of Act III Molière places the third *intermède* (the

cooks' ballet), which sets the scene for a spectacular meal. It is strategically positioned here, quite late in the second movement, to effect a transition from *comédie* to *ballet* and to prepare for their ultimate fusion. The *intermède* introduces a festive mood which arises naturally out of the domestic comedy, and so paves the way for the more fantastical climax to which the movement is now building. There follow two drinking songs, which structurally echo the two songs of the first act. In a dramatic reversal, the festive movement collapses with Mme Jourdain's unwelcome appearance (IV, 2), only to resume almost immediately (IV, 3) with the disguised Covielle arriving to announce the Turkish intrigue. This is the key pivotal point of the play, for in introducing a new *donnée* — a fiction in perfect harmony with M. Jourdain's deepest desires — it serves as a springboard into fantasy. The action then proceeds *accelerando* towards the most elaborate and spectacular *intermède*. In the process, the festive mood aborted in IV, 2 is resumed and quickly transformed into a carnivalesque climate.

The domestic comedy therefore, does not develop independently of the ballet. With the skill of a theatrical connoisseur, Molière orchestrates the different elements, introducing them as required, holding them apart on occasions, before initiating a process of convergence leading to the point where drama and music and dance fuse in a single theatrical image.

Third movement

The Turkish ceremony of Act IV has transformed the play's *données*. M. Jourdain is no longer an aspiring aristocrat, he *is* one, albeit a fictitious one. His initiation to the rank of Mamamouchi completes his journey from obscurity to nobility. In that sense it is the climax and resolution of his particular drama, but the problems he has created along the way remain to be tied up. The remaining business, therefore, is to accommodate the requirements of the action to the new situation. Act V supplies the required dénouement, and does so with considerable brio. The internal structure of Act V follows the classic pattern of the final act of a five-act play, and will be

examined in more detail in chapter 4. Here we are concerned with
the larger structural entity, which presents an apparent problem.

Reading the play, one is aware that the fifth act is short and in
a sense anti-climactic after the Mamamouchi ceremony. The reason
is that Act V completes the play but does not complete the spectacle.
The text reads simply 'La comédie finit par un petit ballet qui avait
été préparé'. This is an enormous understatement. In reality Molière
wrote the play to be accompanied by a very substantial finale, the
Ballet des Nations. It is unfortunate that some editions present only
the play and omit the Ballet des Nations altogether. Although the
livret can give only the most approximate notion of the ballet, it is
central to a proper understanding of the play.

In one sense it is a self-contained set-piece with its own
independent structure, that of a *ballet de cour* with six *entrées*.
Detached from the play, it was performed as a separate ballet at
Court during an entertainment called the *Ballet des Ballets* in 1671.
Nevertheless, the thematic and structural links between the ballet and
the play are greater than is commonly supposed. As in the play,
music, song and dance are introduced cumulatively and are
combined for the finale. Another connection with the play is the
different amorous relationships represented in the ballet. It is also
possible to see a stylised reflection of the play in the movement,
within the ballet, from dissonance and discord to serene good-
humour and harmony.

It begins (1st *entrée*) with a balletic depiction of fractious
disorder. A dancer, attempting to distribute the *livret* to spectators,
moves amongst a swirling multitude of people all babbling in their
various dialects. As with the mock-Turkish of the Mamamouchi
ceremony, familiar sounds can be picked out in the exotic and
strange-sounding chants. This is followed by a more focused variation on the same theme, with three members of the crowd dancing.
The third, fourth and fifth *entrées* introduce the Spanish, Italian and
French companies respectively. Following on from the dance of the
second *entrée*, these *entrées* introduce further media: song (3rd
entrée), musical recitative (4th *entrée*), until finally, for the fifth

entrée, the French musicians dance a minuet and sing. For the sixth *entrée* the *livret* reads:

> Tout cela finit par le mélange des trois nations, et les applaudissements en danse et en musique de toute l'assistance, qui chante les deux vers qui suivent:
> *Quels spectacles charmants, quels plaisirs goûtons-*
> *[nous!*
> *Les Dieux mêmes, les Dieux, n'ont rien de plus doux.*

After the ludicrous posturings of a simple man striving to attain sophistication, the entire *comédie-ballet* is thus crowned by a ravishing spectacle where all the arts unite to present an image of effortless sophistication and elegance. The final couplet is a discreet tribute to *le Roi-Soleil* who presides over such cultural splendour and makes it all possible.

If we are to understand the conception of *Le Bourgeois gentil-homme* it is important to recognise the role of the Ballet des Nations in the overall structure. While it may be excessive to say that the *raison d'être* of the comedy is to prepare for the grand ballet, it is certain that in constructing his play Molière was working towards a substantial ballet as part of the overall scheme. In modern productions the Ballet des Nations is usually omitted or replaced by a very truncated version. This practice can be justified theatrically on the grounds that the *Ballet des Nations* (unlike the *intermèdes*) is not an integral element of the dramatic action, and because of the differing needs and expectations of a modern theatrical performance compared with those of a seventeenth-century *divertissement de cour*. In the context of a whole day given over to Court festivities, the *grand ballet* found a natural place, whereas today it would appear an excessively protracted extension of a theatrical performance. I would argue, though, that even if the *Ballet des Nations* is not performed, the spectacle is structurally and aesthetically incomplete without some final dance to counterbalance the earlier *intermèdes*. Otherwise, the long Turkish *intermède* in Act IV appears as the theatrical climax, making Act V seem insubstantial. A final celebratory dance is also needed as an appropriate expression of the carnival mood on which the play ends.

Interval

There remains the question of an interval. In a conventional play this would be placed between Acts III and IV, but to do so here would be to interrupt the action too obtrusively. The *livret* suggests that breaks were expected after Act II and at some point in Act IV, after the dinner-party but before the Turkish masquerade (*1*, p.232). In modern productions it is customary to place an interval towards the end of Act II, either after scene 13 or possibly after scene 14 when M. Jourdain leaves the stage and before Dorante returns to introduce Dorimène.

Musical structure and dramatic structure

The structural analysis outlined above is based not on the dramatic action but on the spectacle as a whole. Viewed from this angle, it can be seen that the *intermèdes*, far from being decorative appendages, supply the principal punctuation points and climaxes. The musical structure of the spectacle in no way goes against the structure of the play itself. On the contrary, as the following outline will show, when the musical structure is superimposed on the dramatic structure, a perfect match is found.

Again, we must disregard the five-act structure and focus on the main stages of the action. The entire action is centred on M. Jourdain himself and involves his progressive transformation from wealthy bourgeois to *homme de qualité* and finally to Mamamouchi. It is, of course, an entirely imaginary transformation and depends on M. Jourdain's self-ignorance. But simply to dismiss it as imaginary is to ignore, firstly, the fact that as an incorrigible visionary M. Jourdain is unshakeable in the belief in his new identity, and secondly, the manner in which he succeeds in imposing it on everyone else. They may know that M. Jourdain is deluded, but this does not prevent them from being obliged to bow before it to achieve their own ends.

It is customary to describe the central character as gullible and easily deceived by appearances. So he is. Yet it is remarkable how, on another level, he succeeds in making everyone who comes into contact with him dance to his tune. Far from being a simple demonstration of the absurdity of M. Jourdain's notions, the play really portrays a triumph of imagination over reality. The action is organised around the successive stages of a movement from reality to fantasy. Costume plays an important symbolic role in the process. In the course of the play M. Jourdain is seen in three different costumes, corresponding to the three phases of his imaginary metamorphosis.

1. The first phase of the action (Acts I and II) establishes M. Jourdain as the central figure on which the entire edifice is built. In these acts we see him interacting with professionals, all of them exploiting him but, just as importantly, I would say, being used by him to help him fulfil his social aspirations. This phase of the action begins the process whereby he acquires the external trappings (though not, of course, the substance) of the class to which he aspires. It is not by coincidence that it ends with a visual metamorphosis when M. Jourdain exchanges his bourgeois garments for the finery of an *homme de qualité*. The ceremonial enrobing at the end of Act II is a burlesque rite of passage which marks the completion of the first stage of his imaginary transformation.

2. After this extended exposition and reinforcement of M. Jourdain's obsession, Molière then lets him loose on family and acquaintances. The second phase (Acts III and IV) explores the comic consequences of his obsession when pitted against middle-class *bon sens* and aristocratic chicanery. To the extent that M. Jourdain is exposed to ceaseless ridicule, one could say that the action is designed as a corrective to his anti-social behaviour and to prepare his come-uppance. It is a feature of *Le Bourgeois gentilhomme*, however, that the conventional comic structure yields to a different pattern, one which owes more to the logic of fantasy than to the logic of dramatic *vraisemblance*. Instead of working against M. Jourdain's obsession, the characters discover that they must work *with* it, thus allowing him to plunge ever deeper into the

fantasy he has constructed. An early sign of how things will develop is given in III, 13, when Covielle asks Cléonte 'Ne voyez-vous pas qu'il est fou? et vous coûtait-il quelque chose de vous accommoder à ses chimères?' An intrigue, forged from necessity, is therefore set in motion which will lead to M. Jourdain's initiation as Mamamouchi. The second stage of the action thus culminates in another rite of passage where, once again, a new and yet more elevated status is symbolised by a new costume.

3. It is structurally and logically appropriate that the first two stages of the action — M. Jourdain as *bourgeois*, then as *homme de qualité* — should be completed by a third in which M. Jourdain is a titled nobleman. The final stage is a burlesque consecration, in two parts, of M. Jourdain's new identity. It comprises, first, a short fifth act in which the domestic comedy is resolved. Again, there is the paradox that although M. Jourdain cuts an increasingly incongruous and comic figure, the entire *action* (as opposed to what the other characters privately *think*) revolves around an acceptance of his fantasy. His remark as the scene draws to a close, 'Voilà tout le monde raisonnable', affirms the triumph — to his satisfaction — of his fantasy. It remains only for the comedy to be concluded in the traditional manner, with marriages agreed, before the Mamamouchi takes his rightful place of honour to preside over the Ballet des Nations.

Baroque perspective

Superimposed on all this, moreover, is a baroque device whereby the play itself is symmetrically 'framed' by the overture, which leads into the play, and the Ballet des Nations, which leads out of the play and returns it to the context of a *divertissement de cour*. These are integral elements of the performance, without forming part of the play proper, and are no doubt intended consciously to mirror and complement each other. They constitute intermediate levels of reality between the fictitious world represented in the play, and the supposedly 'real' world of the Court entertainment of which it was a part. This framing device is compounded by another intriguing effect, the paradox of infinite regression, or 'chinese box' effect. In the context of the play Dorante is preparing a *divertissement* which he intends to offer to Dorimène. In the event ('voyons notre ballet, et donnons-en le divertissement à Son Altesse Turque' says Dorante), it is to the newly ennobled M. Jourdain that it is offered. In assuming this final role in the comédie-ballet, M. Jourdain burlesques the role of the King. For, in the wider context which embraces the performance, the entire *divertissement* is being offered by the company to Louis XIV. The King, in turn, is offering the spectacle (in which they are all actors) to his Court. The monarch's role as host is reflected in the title-page of the *livret* distributed to spectators, where we read '*Le Bourgeois gentilhomme, comédie-ballet* donné par le Roi à toute sa cour dans le Château de Chambord au mois d'octobre 1670' (*1*, p.230).

By setting a play within a *divertissement* within a Court event, Molière builds the socio-cultural context of the original performance into the structure of the spectacle. The baroque aesthetic, on which all *divertissements de cour* (and indeed Court life itself) ultimately depended, is one which transforms reality into spectacle and illusion. To the extent that it involves self-representation centred on the monarch, it is an aesthetic of royal flattery. This function is plainly reflected in the opera of the period, where the heroic subject matter was implicitly a celebration of the King's exploits. It was intended to be seen as a representation *of* the monarch *to* the monarch, who in turn was part of a spectacle being presented to privileged spectators. In a similar but more subtle way, *Le Bourgeois gentilhomme* reflects the *esthétique de grandeur* of Louis XIV's Court. Without directly alluding to the King, Molière acknowledges the royal presence in the overall structure of the entertainment. It will be useful to bear this perspective in mind when considering Molière's treatment of social themes in the play.

4. Action

In this chapter I shall examine Molière's handling of the action from moment to moment and scene to scene. The reader may therefore find it helpful to have a copy of the text to hand.

In the previous chapter we saw, in broad terms, how Molière constructs a fluid and cohesive entity from the various media of the stage. Close study of the play will now reveal how the action is articulated, and how Molière varies mood and pace to create dramatic and aesthetically pleasing patterns of action. I will show how the playwright combines surprise with a sense of logical inevitability, and how each piece of action slots into place with total apparent naturalness. At the same time, we shall also see recurrent examples of the other hallmark of Molière's theatrecraft, namely the constant pursuit of laughter. It might be thought axiomatic that comedy should be funny, but it was one of Molière's great originalities to have grafted the spirit of farce on to the literary structure of the five-act verse comedy. In the following analysis we shall see the premier technician of laughter at work as he creates and exploits comic opportunities at every turn.

Scene

The stage direction reads 'La scène est à Paris', reminding us that the setting, as so often in Molière's comedies, is the contemporary social environment. Molière's artistic objective, we recall, was to 'faire reconnaître les gens de votre siècle', an aim which scenically implies some degree of topographical realism. The scene is set in a spacious room which would be situated, as was the seventeenth-century practice, on the first floor of M. Jourdain's town house. Whatever stylistic idiom is adopted for the set, it should, of course, signal his status as a wealthy bourgeois.

In accordance with the classical unity of place, the entire action occurs in a single setting which *objectively* does not change. However, this is a comedy in which objective reality is submitted to the distortions of a powerful fantasising imagination. It has already been noted how successive costume changes provide symbolic visual signals of that process. The reader must imagine that the same process will be mirrored by the way in which M. Jourdain transforms his ordinary house into an imaginary palace. At the end of Act III an elaborate banquet has been mounted, while musicians and entertainers are assembling in the *salle basse*, causing Mme Jourdain's indignant protestation: 'Je viens de voir un théâtre là-bas, et je vois ici un banquet à faire noces' (IV, 2). At the end of Act IV the stage takes a further leap into fantasy with the Turkish ceremony. The final, most spectacular transformation occurs at the end of the play when an upstage *ferme* (a movable stage wall) opens to reveal the setting for the Ballet des Nations. M. Jourdain's Parisian home has finally metamorphosed into a fantasy court.

Act I

It is important that both the performance and the play proper begin with music. Lulli's overture and the song which follows serve to acclimatise the audience to a graceful entertainment which charms the senses. We see, and hear, the pupil composing a plaintive serenade ('Je languis nuit et jour...') into which Lulli, with gentle self-mockery, works some precious modulations in the fashionable manner.

The tranquil scene is disturbed by a bustle of movement with the entrance of the musicians and dancers. The first scene has to serve an expository function. But Molière, a master of skilful exposition, imparts the necessary information imperceptibly in a scene which itself contains amusing satire of professional vanity. Both the masters, in subtly nuanced ways, betray a comic contradiction between their inflated dignity and pecuniary greed. When the discussion takes a more personal turn ('je trouve que vous appuyez un peu trop sur l'argent' — 'Vous recevez fort bien pourtant l'argent que notre homme vous donne') there is a hint of the open hostilities which will break out later. A discussion centred on the relationship of artists to a wealthy patron not only introduces a theme of considerable relevance to Molière himself but also establishes why, where and for whom the characters are assembled. Throughout all this, Molière is setting the stage for M. Jourdain's entrance, sketching the outline of his character unambiguously yet tantalisingly. Repeated oblique references to 'il' and 'notre homme', and some more explicit comments ('ce bourgeois ignorant... un homme dont les lumières sont petites') establish the general lines while arousing expectation and curiosity as to the man himself.

The expectations are instantaneously and richly rewarded by M. Jourdain's appearance. A powerful impression of incongruity is conveyed by a man in oriental dressing-gown and nightcap with no less than two lackeys in train. His first words — 'Hé bien, Messieurs? qu'est-ce? me ferez-vous voir votre petite drôlerie?' — immediately stamp him as gauche and uncultured. There follows what appears to be a digression. In reality it is a further revelation of character, motivated by his preoccupation with dress. Socially inept references to his new stockings and his impending new costume reinforce the impression of an irredeemable *esprit bas*, while also establishing the comic preoccupation with self. It is the infallible mark of the monomaniac that he is not only the centre of the action but also demands to be the centre of attention. Indeed, the entire plot, such as it is, will be built upon the consequences of selfish behaviour.

There is a sudden visual shock when he removes the dressing gown to reveal his *déshabillé* (described in the 1671 edition as a green velvet camisole and red velvet *culotte*). This is followed by an extended *lazzo*, a gag in the Italian *commedia dell'arte* style, when M. Jourdain interrupts the musician's song three times to change his dress. It is, however, typical of Molière that the comic gags are not gratuitous farce. They are slipped into the action as revealing character traits. Already the initial realism has given way to comic implausibility, which Molière is not afraid to push to extreme exaggeration. It can safely be assumed that M. Jourdain's comment on the song, 'elle endort', is not merely a metaphorical manner of speaking but a signal that he has been nodding off. In contrast, however, it need not be imagined that M. Jourdain himself sings badly. The humour lies in his unsophisticated choice of a simple rustic air which parodies the languid serenade, and in the reaction of the Masters, both of whom express sycophantic approval.

The antagonism already foreshadowed in the first scene is now developed further when the Masters vie with each other in proclaiming the merits of their respective arts. Molière and his audience would hardly have contested the idea that culture and the arts are indispensable attributes of civilisation. But the Masters' exaggerated self-importance renders their arguments absurd. A special feature of the exchange is its symmetrical structure. The first passage consists of eight *répliques* in four symmetrical couplets. It begins:

M. de M. — La philosophie est quelque chose; mais la musique, Monsieur, la musique...
M. à D. — La musique et la danse... La musique et la danse, c'est là tout ce qu'il faut.

It then builds to a rhetorical crescendo where sound and rhythm replace sense:

M. de M. — Tous les désordres, toutes les guerres qu'on voit dans le monde, n'arrivent que pour n'apprendre pas la musique.
M. à D. — Tous les malheurs des hommes, tous les revers funestes dont les histoires sont remplies, les bévues des politiques, et les manquements des grands capitaines, tout cela n'est venu que faute de savoir danser.

M. Jourdain's terse 'Comment cela?' halts the exchange and initiates the second passage. This is also constructed in couplets but with a different tempo and involving three speakers, following the pattern AB, AB, CB, CB. M. Jourdain's responses — 'Cela est vrai... Vous avez raison... Oui, on dit cela' — supply contrapuntal rhythm, and the movement is finally resolved (in the musical sense) with his triumphant 'Cela est vrai, et vous avez raison tous deux'. The resolution is essential both aesthetically, to complete the sequence, and dramatically, to restore a semblance of harmony in preparation for the forthcoming song.

A formal sequence such as this would seem very artificial in a conventional play. But for the *comédie-ballet*, an inherently artificial genre, Molière has artfully fashioned a rhythmic prose which at certain key moments (this one prepares for the impending 'Dialogue en musique') readily modulates into more stylised sequences. Since Molière deliberately heightens its artificiality, one would expect the stage movements to reflect rather than disguise the symmetry of the dialogue.

Nevertheless, there are limits to the degree of artificiality Molière will tolerate. One line of demarcation which he observes scrupulously is that between dialogue and song. He clearly regarded the operatic conventions of aria and recitative as implausible. He pokes fun at the artificial conventions of the pastoral, with its singing shepherds, by making the Maître à Danser pronounce sententiously: 'Lorsqu'on a des personnes à faire parler en musique, il faut que, pour la vraisemblance, on donne dans le bergerie. Le chant a été de tout temps affecté aux bergers; et il n'est guère naturel en dialogue que des princes ou des bourgeois chantent leurs passions.' In a play which preserves an extremely subtle balance between *vraisemblance* and fantasy, music plays an indispensable role as a conduit from the former to the latter. But never once does Molière introduce music or song gratuitously without justifying them from within the action.

The 'Dialogue en musique' itself is a substantial entertainment in the courtly fashion which is both pleasing for its own sake and a pretext for comedy when M. Jourdain demonstrates boredom. His response 'Est-ce tout?' can be interpreted in several ways, but most plausibly he is seeking reassurance that the music really is over. This would not necessarily be in contradiction with his apparent approval of the piece ('il y là-dedans de petits dictons assez jolis'), which is trite and hardly enthusiastic.

Interest then passes immediately and naturally to the first ballet, to which the Maître à Danser draws M. Jourdain's attention. With perfect transparency, the latter asks wearily 'Sont-ce encore des bergers?', a joke set up earlier by the explanation for the ubiquitous presence of shepherds in the song. It should be said here that the word *intermède* which Molière uses is misleading. It implies a break of some kind, whereas for the spectator it is one link in a continuous chain of action. In fact, the 'Dialogue en musique' and the *intermède* go together as a pair, and are introduced as such earlier by the Maître de Musique ('Voulez-vous voir nos deux affaires?').

Act II

The *intermède*, therefore, is not an interlude but a high point, growing naturally out of the action and leading seamlessly into the following act. M. Jourdain's remark, 'Voilà qui n'est point sot, et ces gens-là se trémoussent bien', is his third crass response to the Masters' offerings, and the last. For Molière builds his comic effects cumulatively in imperceptible stages. So far M. Jourdain has played a spectator's role, supplying humour in his inept responses and comments. In the ensuing scenes he becomes an active participant in a series of lessons and the comedy shifts into a correspondingly higher gear.

Following the *intermède* there is a brief *ralentissement*. Structurally, it allows the dramatic rhythm to catch its breath before launching on the next phase. Molière also uses it to introduce details of the intrigue: the Maître de Musique looks ahead to 'le petit ballet que nous avons ajusté pour vous', and M. Jourdain explains 'la personne pour qui j'ai fait faire tout cela, me doit faire l'honneur de venir dîner céans'. By a perfectly natural progression, this leads to a discussion of M. Jourdain's requirements, the underlying purpose of which is to demonstrate again his social ineptitude. The mood is one of mounting enthusiasm on M. Jourdain's part, which Molière heightens in three stages: 'Il y faudra mettre aussi une trompette marine ... Au moins n'oubliez pas tantôt de m'envoyer des musiciens, pour chanter à table ... Mais surtout, que le ballet soit beau.' By this means Molière is setting him up for the demonstrations of dancing and bowing, which now slip spontaneously into place: 'Ah! les menuets sont ma danse, et je veux que vous me les voyiez danser. Allons, mon maître.' The minuet — 'danse dont les pas sont prompts et petits' (Furetière, *Dictionnaire Universel*) — was highly fashionable in Louis XIV's Court. Molière, therefore, maliciously gives M. Jourdain the most aristocratic and demanding of dances to perform. It is rightly celebrated as a comic *tour de force*, but to appreciate it to the full the reader should if at all possible listen to Lulli's delightful music for the *menuet chanté*.

The comic device of parody is a variation on the earlier scene involving love songs. It is obviously one of the richest resources offered to the comic playwright by the character of the would-be gentleman. It permits clowning, but clowning of the highest order grounded in character and involving 'un ridicule qui se donne en spectacle'. The important element here is not so much M. Jourdain's ostentation itself but the complete absence of self-awareness which accompanies it. Molière instinctively heightens the effect by having M. Jourdain himself draw attention to it: 'je veux que vous me les voyiez danser', and 'Je veux que vous me voyiez faire'. The technique of parody will be used again for the bowing demonstration and the fencing lesson. This appears to be a departure from the unwritten rule of three runs for a joke, but the earlier variation, in Act I, is sufficiently distant for Molière not to appear to be over-exploiting the device.

Capitalising on the heightened comic climate, Molière runs straight from the dance into the next variation, with 'A propos. Apprenez-moi comme il faut faire une révérence pour saluer une marquise'. An expository explanation is slipped into a line of superb comic irrelevance — 'une marquise qui s'appelle Dorimène' — where M. Jourdain's utter transparency is again exposed. Again, Lulli's graceful accompaniment for the bowing provides a perfect framework for an elaborate parody of courtly manners. In contrast, the brusque irruption of the Maître d'Armes (scene 2) introduces a dramatic change of tempo and mood. He thrusts a foil into M. Jourdain's hand and launches without preliminaries into the fencing lesson. The Master's technical instructions contain a forceful rhythm, contrived to produce inescapably comic contortions in the pupil's stance. No doubt they were written to exploit Molière's own highly expressive acting style. Possibilities for comic facial expression ('La tête droite. Le regard assuré') are also accommodated in the text.

The composition of these scenes further reveals Molière's meticulous attention to rhythm. The arrival of the Maître d'Armes has produced a perceptible rise in dramatic tension. The fencing lesson is followed by the requisite *ralentissement*, where he explains the utility of his art (and prompts a further sublimely ridiculous response from M. Jourdain), but it also simultaneously triggers the argument which leads to the next crescendo. The quarrel between the three Masters has a symmetrical configuration which mirrors that of the earlier brief argument (I, 2), but in a heightened dramatic register and more extended form. M. Jourdain's interventions again supply the counterpoint to the alternating responses. Like the earlier dispute, it develops in two stages. In this instance the arrival of the Maître de Philosophie provides a momentary respite, but the movement resumes almost immediately as a four-way argument and continues *crescendo* to the end of scene 3. Once again, the stylised dialogue invites a formal semi-balletic staging.

The recurrent depiction of professional rivalry which motivates the exchanges is enriched by the introduction of a fourth variation on the theme, in the person of the Maître de Philosophie. It is ironic that the stoic philosophy of self-restraint which he preaches causes him, in utter self-contradiction, to come to blows. Bergson, whose theory of laughter arising from mechanical behaviour owed much to his observation of Molière, remarks that a lack of self-awareness lies at the root of much comic behaviour. 'Il n'est pas rare', he notes, 'qu'un personnage comique blâme une certaine conduite en termes généraux et en donne aussitôt l'exemple' (*8*, p.112). The Maître de Philosophie provides a particularly vivid demonstration of that behavioural pattern. The irony is deepened by the fact that the philosophy he expounds is fundamentally admirable. It is undoubtedly right that 'Un homme sage est au-dessus de toutes les injures qu'on lui peut dire; et la grande réponse qu'on doit faire aux outrages, c'est la modération et la patience'. Such behaviour was an essential attribute of the ideal social code known as *honnêteté*. M. Jourdain's own persistent failure to observe it ('je suis bilieux comme tous les diables..' etc.) is yet another instance of the incongruity of his social ambitions. However, Molière is certainly not using the Maître de Philosophie to deliver a lesson in stoic virtue. There is a moral lesson, but it is not a simple precept. It is something altogether more subtle and realistic, and lies in the insight that Molière gives into the limitations of human rationality.

Practical and theoretical considerations prevent the classical stage from being left unoccupied during the action. With the Masters fighting offstage, therefore, Molière leaves M. Jourdain to effect a brief *liaison des scènes*, consoling himself for the collapse of his cultural world with contemplation of his new costume. The monologue also serves to prepare for a return to the conversational mode when the Maître de Philosophie reappears. The quieter extended *scène à deux* (scene 4) is satisfyingly framed by the knock-about scene which precedes it and the busier *habillement* which will bring the act to a spectacular close.

The depiction of the Maître de Philosophie is neatly rounded off by his resumption of the stoic mask as blithely as he discarded it. Thereafter, he reverts to the role of predominantly straight foil to the main comic character as M. Jourdain again assumes centre stage. So far, we have witnessed him attempting, and failing, to master various social attributes which demand skill and grace. But these are mere physical accomplishments. The philosophy lesson, which may owe something to a similar scene in Aristophanes' comedy *The Clouds*, is an extended comic demonstration of his *bassesse d'esprit*. It is, of course, not by chance that this ultimate exposure of M. Jourdain's unfitness for his role has been reserved to the last.

The exposure begins with a rapid survey of the fields of learning. This permits an interplay between a comedy of professional jargon, on the part of the Maître, and a comedy of ignorance on the part of M. Jourdain who finds the proposed topics too ugly (logic), too placid (ethics) or too noisy (physics). The lesson on pronunciation on which he finally settles may appear implausible. In fact, the Master's explanations of how to form the vowels are to be found in a contemporary treatise on grammatical physiology (*Le Discours physique de la parole*, 1668) by Cordemoy, a former tutor to the Dauphin. It provided a perfect model of the futile pedantry which Molière delighted in mocking. He has merely had to modify the text slightly to adjust it to the rhythm of speech and heighten the comic effect. For example, the instruction that *I* should be pronounced 'en... écartant les deux coins de la bouche vers les oreilles' has been added to the original, presumably in order to direct attention to the accompanying grimace. Molière steadily builds the contrast between the pedantic seriousness of the Master and the pupil's naïve delight in the obvious, until the sounds emitted by M. Jourdain transform him into a donkey (I, O, I, O) and a cow (U, U).

Since the *scène à deux* is to be continued, Molière does not on this occasion resolve the sequence with a climax. Instead, he allows it to subside gradually by moving from vowels to consonants. He then uses a further expository line ('Je suis amoureux d'une personne de grande qualité') as the springboard to the comic variations on 'Belle Marquise, vos beaux yeux me font mourir d'amour', by way of the famous lesson on prose. Without extending the lesson unduly (for the scene is now moving towards a conclusion) Molière is content to leave us with the rich irony of M. Jourdain admiring the miracle of prose in a sentence which betrays an irredeemably prosaic mentality: 'Quoi? quand je dis, "Nicole, apportez-moi mes pantoufles, et me donnez mon bonnet de nuit", c'est de la prose?'

M. Jourdain's short monologue following the Maître's departure serves to re-focus the action and prepare for the impending climax. Two earlier allusions to M. Jourdain's new costume, in addition to revealing his innermost preoccupation, have created a sense of anticipation. In the monologue Molière is now staging the final build-up for the scene with the Maître Tailleur. It is at functional moments like these that his attention to detail is most apparent. The short *liaison des scènes* exactly complements and contrasts the earlier one (II, 3-4: see above p.48). As on that occasion, M. Jourdain's mind turns to thoughts of dress, but in contrast to his earlier phlegmatic mood, his mounting impatience with the tailor now produces a comic tantrum. The farcical display of temper is a classic *lazzo*. The appearance of the tailor behind him, at the very moment when he is cursing him, is another.

On one level the scene with the tailor is a continuation of the preceding episodes. The comedy of gullibility completes the character portrait developed during the four lessons, while adding further nuances. In matters of trade, for example, M. Jourdain is perspicacious enough to realise that the Tailor has cheated him, but his *esprit marchand*, unconsciously betraying his origin as the son of a draper, only reinforces his unfitness to be a gentleman. On another level, however, the scene marks a turning point in the action. The various lessons, following a thematic logic already mentioned, have focused attention on attempts to cultivate his social skills and his mind. That they all fail abysmally is richly demonstrated in the lessons themselves, and will be reinforced by further comic exploitations in the following act. The tailor brings this initial phase of the action to an end by transforming M. Jourdain's appearance into that of an *homme de qualité*. The *habillement* itself is not an independent ballet but a heightened dramatic moment with dancing and accompanying music, in which 'Le tout a la cadence de toute la symphonie'. As usual, Molière is careful to introduce it from within the action: 'Mettez cet habit à Monsieur, de la manière que vous faites aux personnes de qualité'. As M. Jourdain liberally dispenses money in return for flattery, the spectator is aware that he is being fleeced. But any unpleasantness is neutralised by M. Jourdain's serene happiness in the fiction, thereby ensuring that the action is brought to an end in a mood of benign good-humour. In exactly the same way as the shepherds' song prepares for the *intermède* at the end of Act I, the dance and the semi-balletic extraction of money lead naturally into the second *intermède*.

Act III

Dramatically this act is one which sets the plot in motion. A related development, on which the plot hinges, concerns the character comedy. The entire first movement has been an extended expository phase which explores facets of a character and an attitude to the world, seen in interaction with a range of professional sycophants. Such dramatic progression as there has been has involved a reinforcement of M. Jourdain's *visions de noblesse*. We are now to see what happens when the *visionnaire* encounters the resistance of the real world. If the play were to follow a conventional comic pattern, one would expect M. Jourdain's absurd and anti-social behaviour to be at least neutralised if not corrected. But Molière's genius in *Le Bourgeois gentilhomme* is to have combined a continuous comic deflation of M. Jourdain's pretensions, with a plot which, paradoxically, allows him to model the world to an ever increasing degree in accordance with his fantasy.

The brief initial scene ('Suivez-moi, que j'aille un peu montrer mon habit par la ville', etc.) provides continuity with the previous act. But with admirable economy Molière also uses it to set M. Jourdain up for the deflation which is to follow, by showing him at his most confident and assertive. The explosion of laughter which greets his appearance is at once an unheeded warning to M. Jourdain, and the fulfilment of the audience's expectations.

Whereas the Masters in the first two acts were extensions of M. Jourdain's world, Nicole is an extension of the audience. The Masters' role was to expose him to ridicule by flattering his pretension; Nicole's is to oppose it. In terms of strict *vraisemblance* she oversteps her social place to deflate M. Jourdain. However, her function is to be understood in terms of a role which belongs not to social reality but to the conventions of comic theatre. The mask of independent-minded and plain-speaking servant, derived from Italian comedy, inspired a whole range of Molièresque servants, from Marotte in *Les Précieuses ridicules* and Dorine in *Tartuffe* to Martine in *Les Femmes savantes*. Molière almost certainly wrote the extended *lazzo* of laughter (scene 2) to exploit the celebrated talent of a new recruit to his company, Mlle Beauval, for producing infectious peals of laughter. The skill with which he develops it has already been observed (see above, p.32). It might be added that a further mark of comic genius lies in judging how far an effect can be exploited and knowing how to end it. In this case Molière extends the hilarity by building to a summit in three stages, then returns to the starting point in order to end it: M. Jourdain giving Nicole her orders neatly causes the laughter to cease as abruptly as it had begun.

Mme Jourdain's arrival (scene 3) gains dramatic impact from being unexpected, but her opening words, 'Ah, ah, voici une nouvelle histoire', pose a question of register for the performer. It is possible that they express the indignation of a no-nonsense character. Alternatively she may be reacting to her husband's appearance in the same way as Nicole, i.e. with the laughter of derision. The question is partly one of intended dramatic effect and partly, of course, one of character. However, the matter cannot be resolved by reference to Mme Jourdain's 'character'. Her character is not a given entity, but is created by the choices made in performance at moments such as this. Critics have tended to assume that Mme Jourdain is intended to supply a perspective of solid middle-class common sense, a role comparable to that of the *raisonneur* in other of Molière's plays. But this is to ignore the fact that Molière wrote the role for the male actor Hubert in 1670. It seems likely that, rather than a socially realistic voice of opposition to her husband, she is intended to produce a dramatic clash of opposites in a burlesque pantomime register.

Molière proceeds to exploit their incompatibility, moving by degrees from *vraisemblance* to pure theatrical farce in a scene which is a masterpiece of cumulative comic effects. Beginning with the bathos of their futile bickering, where M. Jourdain's *visions de noblesse* are undermined by his wife's complaints about the domestic inconvenience they are causing, it progresses to the garbled parody of the philosophy lesson and thence to a high point of farce with the fencing demonstration. At the same time Molière unobtrusively lays expository groundwork for the plot, for the play has reached a point where an intrigue is required to give the action forward momentum.

Mme Jourdain's objection to the domestic turmoil raises in general terms the anti-social consequences of his behaviour. This is shortly to be manifested more concretely in his opposition to Lucile's suitor. Meanwhile, Mme Jourdain's final comment on her husband's behaviour — 'Vous êtes fou, mon mari, avec toutes vos fantaisies, et cela vous est venu depuis que vous vous mêlez de hanter la noblesse' — leads to further bickering about Dorante and so neatly steers the scene from the comic preliminaries to a more active phase of the action. Dorante's timely appearance (scene 4), as if conjured up by the mention of his name, is a feature of theatre rather than life. It is a device used frequently in *Le Bourgeois gentilhomme*, as befits a comedy where a pleasing gratification of expectation is given priority over *vraisemblance*.

Dorante's arrival initiates a return to the comedy of gullibility, echoing that of Acts I and II but with the variation that M. Jourdain here is the willing dupe of an unscrupulous aristocrat. The introduction of the aristocrat completes the social spectrum within the play and offers a telling insight into the mutually parasitic relationship between an impoverished upper class and a wealthy mercantile class. The enumeration of accounts, a comic business used to similar effect in *L'Avare* and *Le Malade imaginaire*, proceeds at a forceful rhythm to a climax which explodes into laughter with Dorante's insouciant request for more money. The comedy of M. Jourdain's fleecing is further enriched by the presence of Mme Jourdain, first as disapproving witness, then in asides which draw him into discordant squabbling. Silent reinforcement of her position is supplied by Nicole whose presence permits mimed interaction with Mme Jourdain. The situation is brought to a head with M. Jourdain torn between obsequious conversation with Dorante and unseemly bickering with his wife. His discomfiture symbolically demonstrates his self-inflicted isolation, unwilling to belong in one social class and unfitted to belong in the other.

The scene is resolved by M. Jourdain going off-stage to find money for Dorante. His absence, although given a logical justification, is really engineered to permit Molière to stage the skirmish (scene 5) between Dorante and Mme Jourdain. As well as introducing a pleasing variation in tempo, this allows the restrained hostility between them to be aired further in an intriguing exchange between two people who socially have nothing in common. Dorante's dubious compliment to Mme Jourdain on her attractive appearance, coupled with a reference to her age, may be inadvertently tactless. If not, Dorante must be taunting her with barely disguised insults. The question is an important one, for upon it hinges not only the interpretation of Dorante's character but also the light it casts on the class he represents. Is Dorante a shrewdly calculating interloper, aware that in order to achieve his ends he need only cultivate M. Jourdain while riding roughshod over the rest of the household? Or is he a good-humoured impecunious aristocrat doing what comes naturally, and what society condones, without consulting his conscience too deeply? The text does not provide an answer. However, if one recalls that in 1670 his remarks to Mme Jourdain were addressed to a middle-aged male actor, a burlesque effect rather than one of black comedy seems more likely. Dorante's aristocratic elegance, while providing a fine contrast to his adversary's frank rudeness, ensures that the conversation preserves some veneer of civility. Nevertheless, M. Jourdain's reappearance is a welcome relief in the strained atmosphere.

Molière now turns his attention to the plot. It is a distinctive and sometimes criticised feature of *Le Bourgeois gentilhomme* that it disregards the conventional wisdom which demanded that the main facts be expounded early in the play. Molière could easily have done so in this case, but he evidently chose not to. Presumably he judged that in *Le Bourgeois gentilhomme*, where plot is not the main organising principle, it was dramatically advantageous to introduce information only as and when it was required. Any possible loss in terms of the overall tightness of the plot is more than compensated by the fresh dramatic impetus that comes from the injection of a new element. Scene 6 is therefore essentially concerned with preparing for Dorimène's entertainment, an exposition which Molière lards with comic business in the form of eavesdropping and asides. It culminates farcically in a slap and is resolved with a hasty exit in which M. Jourdain attempts to salvage his dignity. Another short scene (scene 7) introduces a further expository strand ('Mais songeons à ma fille. Tu sais l'amour que Cléonte a pour elle...'). Repeating the device by which Dorante was conjured up, the reference to Dorante and Covielle causes them to burst upon the scene.

The episode which follows (scenes 9-10), containing the *dépit amoureux* or lovers' quarrel, is a conventional set-piece. That it does nothing to advance the action is true, since it is not intended to do so. But it is certainly not mere padding to fill out a slender intrigue, as Adam claims (*6*, p.383), nor is it gratuitous. Its structural necessity relates not to any contribution to the action itself, but to the fact that the ensuing plot is built on an obstacle to the lovers' marriage: it is therefore necessary for the playwright to engage the spectators' interest in their fate. Given that necessity, he fulfils it with a piece of sentimental comedy which, when properly performed, is charming and captivating. The *dépit amoureux* was a recognised theatrical convention which featured in many comedies of the period including some of Molière's. But if the concept is unoriginal, the manner of its treatment is entirely Molière's own and demonstrates his genius in tailoring his material to the medium. The doubling of couples, making the servants caricature the masters, is one original feature of this version. And, since this is *comédie-ballet*, Molière does not present the episode naturalistically. Instead, he emphasises its artificiality, giving it the formal structure of a dance. It is, in effect, another little ballet within the comedy-ballet but, instead of being set to music, the movements and rhythm are supplied in the dialogue. This is not to say that the sequence should be mechanically stylised. The intended effect is a more delicate one created by a blend of apparent spontaneity within a pattern of harmonised movements.

The fact that such scenes belonged to stock convention frees the playwright from the need to introduce it plausibly. Nevertheless, it should be noted that Molière works towards it by subtle changes of rhythm and tempo which heighten the artificiality in stages. The process is initiated, imperceptibly, in scene 6 where, although there is no formal pattern to the dialogue, the situation of opposing pairs of characters will naturally lead the actors to take up opposing positions on the stage. Then, starting from the conversational mode in scene 7, the dialogue passes through an unobtrusively symmetrical exchange between Nicole and the two men in scene 8, and thence into the complete symmetry of scene 9. From there it is only a short step to the full quadrille in scene 10. With Nicole and Covielle parodying Lucile and Cléonte in a minor key, the two couples execute patterns of distancing and convergence in perfect symmetry, until the eventual explanations dispel the misunderstanding and initiate a progressive return to a more natural conversational mode.

With the lovers reconciled the action resumes at a rapid pace. Mme Jourdain's timely reappearance, followed immediately by that of her husband, bring matters to a head. With the question of the father's consent to his daughter's marriage we are on the familiar terrain common to many of Molière's comedies. The outcome is wholly predictable, but Molière contrives to make it unexpected. A climate of optimism has been created at the end of scene 10, and it is reinforced by Mme Jourdain's encouragement in scene 11. Cléonte's admirable demonstration of his qualities as an *honnête homme* further underlines his obvious suitability as a partner for Lucile. The puncturing of this hopeful climate is rendered more dramatic by a misunderstanding: M. Jourdain's proffered hand, with his reply, 'Touchez-là, Monsieur', are an unexpected but welcome sign taken to indicate consent, but are followed after the briefest of pauses by 'Ma fille n'est pas pour vous'.

It can now be seen that Molière has brought this strand of the intrigue to a *noeud* in a rapid and dramatic manner. But the resulting situation is a particularly problematic one for the comic playwright, for it threatens to plunge the play from comedy into pathos. It is doubtless for this reason that he does not focus on the lovers' plight, nor allow them to voice their reaction. Instead he restores a comic climate by engaging M. Jourdain in an exchange of recriminations with his wife. By the same token his potentially repellent selfishness — 'Ne me répliquez pas davantage, ma fille sera marquise en dépit de tout le monde' — is rounded off with an absurd comic flourish on the exit line: 'et si vous me mettez en colère, je la ferai duchesse'.

The same concern to maintain an optimistic climate dominates scene 13. Cléonte must contemplate the impasse he has reached, but

Molière transposes it to a humorous register by allowing the servant to deliver a rebuke to the master: 'Vous avez fait de belles affaires avec vos beaux sentiments'. He then immediately steers attention towards the counter-measures to be adopted. Covielle's observation of the need to 'vous accommoder à ses chimères' provides a pointer to the direction the action will take. Covielle's role, like Nicole's, is one shaped by theatrical tradition. The mask of nimble-witted valet (Coviello in the *commedia dell'arte*, and servants such as Sganarelle in *Le Médecin malgré lui*) allows Covielle to slip into the role of *meneur du jeu* as he outlines his plan of action to Cléonte.

From this point the action gathers speed and complexity. Leaving the Cléonte-Lucile intrigue in suspension, Molière now develops the second intrigue. A momentary reappearance by M. Jourdain (scene 14) may appear redundant, but it serves to re-focus attention on his relations with the aristocratic couple and, for clarity, allows the *laquais* to introduce the latter by name. With Dorimène's arrival the cast is complete. Scene 15 is basically expository, whilst also setting up business (for example, the misunderstanding over the diamond) to be exploited later. In itself it is not comic, though it provides some wry amusement from the realisation of the precise way in which M. Jourdain is being exploited by Dorante. His role in the intrigue is unambiguous. Dorimène's is probably intended to be no less so, though much ink has been spilled over the centuries concerning her involvement in a dubious enterprise (see 49). An objective reading of the scene suggests that it is intended to characterise her as basically honest, an unwitting accomplice in an intrigue devised by Dorante. If we accept this, then what Molière is giving us is not a 'couple d'aventuriers de haut vol' (*11*, p.278), but something more nuanced: a model of genuine aristocratic *honnêteté*, to set against Dorante's abuse of the same and M. Jourdain's burlesque imitation of the real thing.

After this quieter interlude M. Jourdain's entrance in scene 16 restores a climate of farce. Seeing Dorimène, he launches immediately into the *lazzo* which was prepared in II, 1. The elaborate parody of a triple bow is a classic illustration of Bergson's theory of comic *raideur*: M. Jourdain mechanically executes the movement he has been taught, conscientiously ignoring the fact that the situation makes it impossible. It gives a physical manifestation of the linear conduct that marks the behaviour of a monomaniac. The remainder of the scene gives the impression of aimless badinage, but that is partly the point. M. Jourdain has been placed in an archetypal situation, that of the host receiving guests for a dinner-party, which will test his social skills to the limit. Molière makes the two guests interact to extract a double comic effect. Dorimène elicits a clumsy string of tongue-tied compliments, while the interspersed asides with Dorante prolong the comedy of gullibility.

The act began by showing the would-be gentleman in domestic company, and ends by showing him in aristocratic company. The result in both cases is identical: comic deflation. But whereas the opening scene subjected him to the raucous laughter of a servant, the last scene exposes him to a more sophisticated teasing. The effect is a good-humoured but somewhat strained atmosphere of anticipation. It leads naturally to the timely and welcome appearance of the banquet, which installs a more festive mood. The cooks' ballet, although an *intermède*, is again staged from within the action, and leads directly into the action in the following act.

Act IV

Structurally, Molière's main concern in the fourth act is to maintain the forward movement of the action and to propel it towards a climax. The two intrigues that have been initiated are both brought to a head, giving the act a pattern which is dramatically exciting and aesthetically satisfying. Molière brings the secondary intrigue to a rapid climax (scene 1) and disposes of it in a dramatic collapse (scene 2). Without a pause, he re-introduces the primary intrigue (scene 3) which quickly acquires its own momentum (scene 4), culminating in the summit (scene 5) which is both a spectacular climax to the act and the apotheosis of the fantasy towards which the play has built.

The opening exchange of words provides a functional liaison with the preceding *intermède*. M. Jourdain's reply to Dorimène's compliment, which he takes to be addressed to himself, is a characteristically clumsy attempt at *galanterie*. It also further underlines the comic ambiguity of the situation, an effect which Dorante revels in exploiting in his own more inspired piece of gallantry. His ornate speech evoking an imaginary meal is a sustained precious conceit. It reflects the seventeenth-century aristocratic ideal of wit, and is perhaps the only moment in the play that is really dated for modern tastes. However, it allows one to measure the distance between M. Jourdain's platitudinous attempts at wit and Dorante's effortless urbanity. More generally, it evokes the unattainable sophistication to which M. Jourdain aspires in a culture where even eating and drinking are refined into an elaborate culinary art.

As on previous occasions, Molière marks the impending highpoint with a musical *ornement*. The drinking songs provide a structural counterpart to the two songs in Act I, but in a register to harmonise with the context. Again, they are not in the least gratuitous. Springing naturally out of the action, they also offer a witty musical commentary on the action itself. The first, sung by a lover to his mistress, contains a charmingly sensuous invocation to pleasure, and it is followed by one whose moral might be resumed as 'gather ye rosebuds while ye may'. They parody in advance the amorous *quiproquo* when, encouraged by the mood-expanding songs, M. Jourdain launches on a series of compliments to the *marquise*, each one more bold than the last. Dorimène's good-humoured response to the incongruity, as it seems to her, of his efforts at *galanterie*, encourages M. Jourdain towards a full-blown declaration of passion, which is anticipated in his fourth, interrupted, *réplique*: 'Si je pouvais ravir votre coeur, je serais...'

Mme Jourdain's inopportune appearance at this moment is as sudden as her earlier one (III, 3). As before, it combines inevitability and surprise for dramatic effect. At one level it comes as a shock, an effect reinforced by her prolonged absence from the action and the increasingly unreal festive climate that has been created. On another level, however, it is a predictable fulfilment of the audience's expectations. For this is comedy. And, if a characteristic feature of tragedy is that two people who should be brought together fail to

meet, the classic situation of comedy is that characters who should
be kept apart are brought together.

Her opening words, 'Ah, ah! je trouve ici bonne compagnie',
mirror those of III, 3, but this time there is no possible ambiguity:
she is indignant, as the situation warrants. This is not, however,
without danger for the comedy. A *trouble-fête* spoiling the fun risks
being unwelcome, and a wronged wife defending her legitimate
interests, if taken seriously, belongs more to drama than to comedy.
A burlesque interpretation of the role will redress matters, but
Molière is also careful to steer the action back to comic territory.
Dorante's protestation of innocence (a deception which Dorante and
M. Jourdain, for their own different reasons, are both keen to
sustain) is a diversionary tactic that belongs to comedy. Mme
Jourdain's plain-speaking abuse of the aristocratic guests produces
comic discomfiture for their host, modulating to comic despair at
Dorimène's flight and comic rage when he turns on his wife. The
bathos is completed by the removal at this point of the banquet table,
visually reinforcing the collapse of M. Jourdain's dream.

M. Jourdain is left on stage to effect the *liaison des scènes*, and
to give us another glimpse of his self-deception as he regrets his
unspoken witticisms. Molière now switches to the main intrigue,
with the perfectly timed arrival of Covielle. Rational argument
having been tried and shown to fail (III, 12), other methods must be
used to deflect M. Jourdain — not to cure him, but simply to ensure
the marriage. The solution, simple and inspired, lies not in recourse
to a *deus ex machina* external agent, but within M. Jourdain himself.
If the *visionnaire*'s credulity and capacity for self-deception make
him a willing dupe of malicious schemers, the same qualities can be
turned to good effect by his family. That is what Covielle now
proceeds to exploit. Mme Jourdain's earlier remark about Dorante's
handling of M. Jourdain, 'Il le gratte par où il se démange', applies
perfectly to this situation too. Covielle's fiction concerning M.
Jourdain's noble birth draws him to the bait, and the apparently
casual question 'Vous savez que le fils du Grand Turc est ici?'
impales him on the hook. The speed with which the scene develops

is a factor in its acceptance, with M. Jourdain progressing rapidly from surprise through stupefaction to unbridled rapture.

Molière's debt to Italian improvised comedy is apparent in the episode of Covielle's *bourle*. The *burla*, or practical joke, was a classic feature of a *commedia dell'arte* scenario. Often it took the form of a punishment, at its simplest a beating, perpetrated on a self-centred older man by a servant in league with young lovers. Molière's genius in *Le Bourgeois gentilhomme* is to have worked the traditional function of the *bourle* into character comedy so that, whilst administering the expected punishment, and in doing so achieving their own ends, they are also giving M. Jourdain what he thinks he wants.

The groundwork has been laid so that nothing will now impede the action from advancing rapidly towards the *turquerie*. Molière gives us a first glimpse of Cléonte dressed as a Turk (scene 4) and uses M. Jourdain's absence to re-introduce Dorante as an observer (scene 5). Almost immediately the music strikes up and Turks appear. Structurally the *turquerie* constitutes the fourth *intermède*. Like the previous ballets, it is not an interlude but an integral piece of the action. As well as marking a key point in the dramatic development, it lays the foundation of the future dénouement.

It is the longest and most elaborate ballet within the play, with four dervishes and twelve other Turks on stage together with the Mufti and M. Jourdain. The costumes and turbans were made by the company's tailor Baraillon, under the supervision of the Chevalier D'Arvieux (*7*, p.252). D'Arvieux also played an important role in suggesting elements of Turkish ritual. Its sources are not without historical interest (see *39*), but, of course, the real significance of the Turkish ceremony is theatrical. Molière and Lulli surpassed themselves to devise a comic *tour de force*. Outlandish costumes, music and dance combine with the pseudo-Turkish incantations (actually a form of *lingua franca* known as 'sabir') to create ten minutes of sublime ridicule. Lulli's music, introducing exotic instruments and rhythms into a classical framework, includes a march, four dances and numerous chants. It is the perfect accompaniment to the burlesque ceremonial and lends itself to much expressive gesture and grimace. As well as composing the music, Lulli helped to devise the dances. He also played the part of the Mufti, which in the 1670 production was very substantial. A contemporary wrote 'Il chanta lui-même le personnage du Mufti, qu'il exécutait à merveilles [sic]. Toute sa vivacité, tout le talent naturel qu'il avait pour déclamer se déployèrent là... Le Roi, qu'il divertit extrêmement, lui en fit des compliments' (1, p.178).

The original ballet (not performed in its entirety after 1670) has an independent structure, starting with a ceremonial entry and passing through the various stages of an initiation ritual. After the opening march, the scene is set with preparatory chanting and dancing ('Le Mufti invoque Mahomet'). M. Jourdain is then brought in dressed *à la turque*, but minus the turban. The Mufti sings his first address to M. Jourdain ('Se ti sabir' etc.) where the novice is asked to identify himself if he understands, or else remain silent. Not surprisingly, M. Jourdain remains silent. The Mufti then sings the questions to the dervishes, who chant replies on M. Jourdain's behalf. Turning to M. Jourdain again, he prepares him for his initiation: 'Mahametta per Giourdina' etc. (i.e. 'Soir et matin je prierai Mahomet pour Jourdain. Je veux faire un Paladin de Jourdain. Je lui donnerai turban et sabre, avec galère et brigantine, pour défendre la Palestine'). Then comes a second interrogation, 'Star bon Turca Giourdina?' ('Jourdain est-il bon Turc?'), with the dervishes again chanting the responses, this time in Turkish, 'Hi valla' ('Oui, par Dieu').

At this point there is a dramatic change of tempo when the Mufti and his assistants launch into a mad dance, chanting 'Hou la ba ba' as they encircle M. Jourdain. This creates a sense of impending climax, as well as underlining the isolation of an increasingly terrified M. Jourdain. The Turks now perform another ceremonial dance, followed by more chanted prayers, before the third and final interrogation: 'Ti non star fourba, Non star furfanta' ('Tu n'est pas fourbe? Tu n'est pas fripon?'). The preliminaries over, the ceremony now advances to the act of initiation. First there is another dance: 'Le Mufti et les Dervis se coiffent avec des turbans de cérémonie, et l'on présente au Mufti l'Alcoran, qui fait une seconde invocation'. In

1670 the comic effect of the first action was increased by the use of absurdly large turbans. According to the 1682 text, Lulli's was decorated with four or five rows of lighted candles (*1*, p.189). For the latter action, which consists of pounding the Koran, the book is placed on the initiate's back, constituting a first *bastonnade* for M. Jourdain. The Mufti sings 'Ti star nobile' etc. ('Tu est noble, ce n'est pas un mensonge. Prends ce sabre'). In the fourth dance, dervishes brandishing sabres encircle M. Jourdain, 'auquel ils feignent de donner plusieurs coups de sabre'. This leads into the *bastonnade*, where the assistants are encouraged by the Mufti chanting 'Dara dara bastonnara'. A *reprise* of the third dance acts as an interlude before the Mufti's final invocation to the new Mamamouchi, 'Non tener honta / Questa star ultima affronta' ('N'aie pas honte, ceci est le dernier affront'). M. Jourdain's ludicrous situation is underlined by the ironic play on the double meaning of 'ultima' (ultimate and last).

The Mamamouchi's initiation is now complete, but in the original version the *intermède* continues with numerous *reprises* of chants and dances, and finally returns to the opening march. The amazing hallucinatory spectacle is still in progress when Mme Jourdain comes upon the scene, bringing it to a sudden halt and opening the final act.

Act V

Where the plot is concerned, Molière now has his sights set on resolving the conflict between M. Jourdain and the other characters, a conflict focused specifically on the obstacle to the lovers' marriage. Resolving that problem will constitute the dénouement. The previous act, as well as producing a great comic climax, has prepared for its resolution but the problem itself remains to be solved. The final act combines the necessary dénouement with exploitation of comic effects made possible by M. Jourdain's new condition. In the classic manner, Molière suspends the action in order to delay the dénouement until the very last moments of the play. A similar pattern is commonly found in tragedy, where the final catastrophe is preceded by a suspenseful pause, and in other comedies by Molière. A particularly good example is *Tartuffe* where, as in *Le Bourgeois gentilhomme*, the dramatic movement is held in suspension by scenes which do nothing to advance the plot but milk the comic potential of the new situation.

The act begins as a *reprise* of Act III. M. Jourdain, newly attired in an outlandish costume, is subjected to a series of deflationary encounters. For the third time (cf. III, 3 and IV, 2) Mme Jourdain bursts upon her husband when his mind is filled with visionary notions, producing a comic collision between characters living on divergent planes of reality. As before, Molière exploits the comic device of parody with the central character enacting a garbled version of earlier action. Comedy of non-communication, already present in the previous versions of this situation, attains a new high point with M. Jourdain repeating the incantations of the Turkish mascarade. In the 1670 performance, Molière's mimicry of Lulli's distinctive high-pitched singing voice must have added special spice, especially if it was an accurate imitation. The demonstration culminates in a farcical climax when M. Jourdain burlesques the 'hou la ba ba' dance. The 1682 edition adds the stage direction '*et tombe par terre*'. Whether this is a recollection of Molière's performance, or of a more recent production such as that at the Guénegaud theatre (1680) one cannot say. In any event, M. Jourdain's collapse would aptly echo the fall that followed his demonstration of fencing techniques in III, 3. Throughout this farcical self-condemnation, M. Jourdain remains true to his comic essence, his lack of self-awareness intact. In this and the following scenes, Molière reveals the essential isolation of the monomaniac as he withdraws further into his cocoon of fantasy. This is why it is so perfectly apt that, instead of bickering with his wife as previously, the imaginary *grand seigneur* now treats her with attempted disdain. His magisterial exit-line, 'Paix! insolente, portez respect à Monsieur le *Mamamouchi*', presents a complete image of untouchable self-delusion.

Weaving the remaining threads together, Molière re-introduces Dorante and Dorimène (scene 2). A short scene of rational rather than passionate courtship anticipates their marriage. After the necessary business is concluded, M. Jourdain's return restores the comic climate. Scene 3 supplies the necessary complement to scene 1: having exposed the new Mamamouchi to his family entourage in the first scene, Molière now exposes him to the aristocratic entourage. This double process exactly parallels that of Act III. The garbled and nonsensical versions of Turkish greetings, as well as continuing from scene 1 the parody of the Turkish ceremony, also recall M. Jourdain's clumsy salutations to Dorimène in III, 16. Parody modulates into farce after the appearance of Cléonte (scene 4) with M. Jourdain's frustrated attempts to communicate in Turkish without the help of the *truchement*.

With the return of the remaining characters (scenes 5 & 6), the action acquires the unmistakable feel of a build-up towards a theatrical grand finale. The outcome is clearly anticipated, but Molière injects dramatic suspense by means of the *quiproquo*. Ironically, it is now Lucile who refuses to marry Cléonte, understandably enough in view of his disguise. Her sudden change of heart when she recognises Cléonte, with no attempt by Molière to make it plausible, underlines both the theatricality of the situation and M. Jourdain's gullibility in his acceptance of it. Mme Jourdain's objection, in scene 6, repeats the device in an expanded form. A masterly construction of the dialogue helps to extract maximum dramatic and comic effect from the situation. The various characters' interventions have something of the stylised pattern of earlier symmetrical exchanges. The dialogue proceeds *accelerando* to a plateau, marked by 'Hé bien! quoi?' It is held in suspense during Covielle's whispered explanation, and released in an inescapably comic resolution when she affirms her consent. The sequence, and the entire action, is then crowned by M. Jourdain's 'Ah! voilà tout le monde raisonnable', demonstrating how total is the inversion of rational norms. It remains only for the two other marriages to be announced — the conventional conclusion to a comedy — before all the characters, entering into the spirit of M. Jourdain's 'reasonableness', take their seats for the *divertissement*. The action then runs without a break into the Ballet des Nations.

5. Significance

The meaning of comedy

The playwright Harold Pinter once remarked that the theatre is not a branch of the Post Office, by which he meant that its job is not to deliver messages. It would certainly be futile to attempt to reduce a play as exuberant and subtle as *Le Bourgeois gentilhomme* to a closed set of meanings with an unequivocal message. This is not to say, as has occasionally been suggested, that the comedy is meant to function only on the level of entertainment. Riotous fun it may be, but spectators who enter into the spirit of Molière's comic vision will find it no less rich in significance than his more markedly philosophical comedies. Whatever Molière's intentions were when he wrote the play (which in any case are unknowable), it is in fact a work of great social and psychological perception.

Like all works of art, the play suggests a vision of life, and that vision in turn implies an attitude to the world. It could hardly be otherwise. All comedy is serious to the extent that it expresses an awareness of imperfection in life. In a hypothetical perfect world, there could be no comedy because there would be nothing to laugh at. The real world, which is Molière's starting point, is plainly not perfect. Many things go amiss, notably people who can be foolish and blind, with consequences which are both serious and comic.

Interpretation of Molière in recent years has tended to stress the moral irresponsibility of comedy. It has become a commonplace to remark that the function of comedy is not to make judgements. A representative of this tendency, René Bray, writes: 'Molière n'a pensé qu'à nous faire rire ... l'intention de Molière, la pensée qui donne à son oeuvre la force et l'unité, ce n'est pas une pensée de moraliste, c'est une intention d'artiste' (*17*, pp.22 and 36). Bray is no doubt right to stress that Molière's plays are primarily comic structures not moral theorems. And it is true that Molière does not force us to make simple choices between right and wrong. Often the opposition is between two flawed attitudes, as between the irresponsible free-thinking of Dom Juan and the uninformed credulity of Sganarelle. A similar ambiguity arises in *Le Misanthrope* from the opposition between Alceste, with his rigid and unsociable virtue, and those more sociable people whom he justifiably criticises for their moral laxity.

But to say that comedy is morally ambiguous is not to say that it is morally neutral. Satire obviously implies criticism, and laughter in general is often thought to be a form of punishment. According to Bergson, laughter operates as a 'social gesture' whose function is to reprimand unsociable behaviour. In the seventeenth century a similar idea was expressed in the formula *castigat ridendo mores*. In fact, no-one has ever succeeded in demonstrating that laughter's supposed corrective function is effective in causing people to modify their behaviour. It seems highly improbable that Molière really believed that potential Jourdains and Dorantes would be reformed by exposure to ridicule. All the evidence in the play suggests not. If there is a lesson, it is to be understood not in the narrow sense of prescriptions for good behaviour but in terms of promoting a more accurate perception of the world.

Human nature

Applying these thoughts to *Le Bourgeois gentilhomme*, one aspect of the lesson, rather obviously, is the portrayal of character. In keeping with the humanist preoccupations of the classical age, Molière was profoundly interested in human nature. He shows the individual mind as a battle-ground between reason and unreason. At the core of the play, and central to any lesson it might contain, is an *idée fixe*. M. Jourdain's eccentric behaviour is centred on his social pretensions, but these are not its ultimate source. His aspirations are so incongruous, so utterly discordant with his reality, that they amount to a kind of perversity which can be explained only by a fundamental absence of common sense. Such exemplary comic blindness provides a case-book illustration in the negative of Descartes's definition of *le bon sens* as 'la puissance de bien juger et distinguer le vrai d'avec le faux'.

Through his depiction of an individual in the grip of an *idée fixe*, Molière deepens our understanding of the irrational side of the human psyche. This pleasurable lesson depends for its effectiveness on a sense of recognition. The process by which it is achieved merits some comment One aspect of the celebrated realism of Molière's comedy, and perhaps his greatest artistic achievement, lies in presenting us with a compelling illusion of character, so vivid and lifelike that we are forced to recognise the accuracy of the portrait. But to say simply that his depiction of M. Jourdain is psychologically realistic is misleading. The character, obviously, is not a real person but a theatrical illusion. One of the paradoxes of the make-believe art of theatre is that real objects, real furniture, look flat and false. On the stage, only the artificial looks real. Seventeenth-century writers were aware of this effect when they framed the idea of *vraisemblance* — literally 'true-seeming' rather than 'real'. The paradox applies with no less force to the notion of character. Where the invention of character is concerned, the artistic process by which life is transposed into theatre involves simplification and exaggeration. We have seen how Molière, starting from a basically plausible situation, soon abandons verisimilitude in favour of comic exaggeration. From any naturalistic perspective, gestures such as pushing Dorimène to make room for his bow are unrealistic. But in the heightened theatrical register of the comedy they are truthful expressions of his fundamental nature. In the process, the individual becomes a type, that is to say a chemically pure essence of the *bourgeois gentilhomme*. It is this distillation of behaviour into an archetype that makes M. Jourdain, son of a seventeenth-century Parisian draper, instantly familiar to audiences of all centuries.

The individual and society

As well as heightening our awareness of the irrational, the comedy explores the precarious relationship between the individual and collective life. Like his contemporaries, Molière took it for granted that man's natural milieu was urban society. It is, therefore, man as a social animal, situated in a precise social environment at a given historical moment, that is the object of his observations.

Social life implies a measure of adaptability. It demands some submission of the individual to the rules of collective behaviour. This may be considered oppressive, a means of subjugating the individual to the dominant values of the time. Alternatively it may be seen, as it commonly was in Molière's day, as simply a necessary requirement of civilised life. In the seventeenth century, social conformism was encapsulated in the concept of *honnêteté*, an ideal code of behaviour based on moderation, common sense and tact. Molière's heroes, however, in defiance of social requirements, are extreme individualists. Their non-compliance makes them socially disruptive because their obsessions threaten the interests of others. It is not by accident that his plays are constructed in such a way as to highlight not only the character of the obsession but also its consequences for other people. Two frequent consequences of monomania, both of them illustrated in *Le Bourgeois gentilhomme*, are gullibility (a product of blindness) and selfishness, frequently expressed in an insistence against all common sense to marry one's daughter to the wrong person. It is the immediate family entourage which bears the direct brunt of this misbehaviour. But insofar as the family is a microcosm of society and the basic unit of middle-class life, obsessive behaviour can be seen as having threatening implications for society as a whole.

The tension between society and its individual members is as actual today as in seventeenth-century France. Molière traces its source to a fundamental self-centredness in man, but supplies no answer to the problem, because none is realistically possible. In *Le Bourgeois gentilhomme*, of course, the immediate problem is resolved to the satisfaction of all parties, but we are well aware that this is a theatrically contrived ending. In real life, where there are no theatrical dénouements, the problems created by foolish behaviour admit of no simple solution. The play implicitly recognises this by presenting M. Jourdain's *idée fixe* as an incurable condition.

Class

In *Le Bourgeois gentilhomme* the general theme of social relations is linked to a more specific issue, that of class. Social snobbery is no doubt a universal trait, but for Molière's contemporaries the noble pretensions of a rich *parvenu* were a subject of immediate topical interest. By the 1670s the figure was evidently sufficiently common to constitute a social archetype. La Fontaine immortalised the type in a number of fables, including that of the Rat and the Elephant, where he writes:

> Se croire un personnage est fort commun en France.
> On y fait l'homme d'importance,
> Et l'on n'est souvent qu'un bourgeois:
> C'est proprement le mal François.

Spectators today will have no difficulty in recognising a class-ridden society where money and taste are not synonymous. This is enough to make the general situation self-explanatory for modern audiences. For that reason I have concentrated in this study on comic and dramatic structures and allowed the context to speak for itself. Readers who require more information should consult an article by David Shaw where the play is related in detail to its social background (*48*). Here, I will confine my discussion to some comments on Molière's treatment of the theme of class.

His social canvas is actually quite restricted. Not unnaturally, the social environment on which he concentrates is that of his own theatre-going public. The milieu depicted is that of an urban élite, encompassing the wealthy middle class and outer Court circles, but completely ignoring the peasantry who constituted by far the largest class numerically. Within this range, though, and making due allowance for comic distortion, the play gives a remarkably accurate and nuanced picture of contemporary class structures. The fact of M. Jourdain's wealth, coupled with his social aspirations, places him naturally at the centre of a web of relations representing a spectrum of social conditions from servants to nobility.

Seen from a distance, Louis XIV's France presents the appearance of a monolithic, stable hierarchy ordered from above by the system of absolutism. In reality, society was more mobile, and probably more unstable, than one might suppose. In the play this is suggested by the declining fortunes of the aristocracy and the unsatisfactory situation of the rising mercantile class envying the prestige of its superiors. Molière exploits this to comic effect by bringing together the *bourgeois* who has money without prestige, and the aristocrat who has prestige but no money — opposite poles of a magnet, comically and inevitably attracted to each other in pursuit of their self-interest.

In society, the adjective *bourgeois* could have a pejorative flavour, as is shown by this entry in Furetière's dictionary (1690): '*Bourgeois*: se dit quelquefois en mauvaise part par opposition à un homme de la Cour, pour signifier un homme peu galant, peu spirituel, qui vit et raisonne de la manière du bas peuple.' In *Les Femmes savantes* an insult is obviously intended when Bélise says of Chrysale 'Est-il (...) un esprit composé d'atomes plus bourgeois?' (II, 7, v.617). But *Le Bourgeois gentilhomme* also reflects the fact that the bourgeoisie itself, far from being a homogeneous class, embraced a range of *conditions* from merchants and tradesmen (like M. Jourdain's father and father-in-law), professionals of various kinds (such as the four parasitic Maîtres), to the officers of state occupying a range of administrative posts to which varying degrees of distinction were attached. There is a point, exemplified by Cléonte, where the more prestigious end of this particular social scale shades into nobility. It is one of the play's ironies that Cléonte, with his parents 'qui ont tenu des charges honorables' and his six years of service 'dans les armes' (a touchstone of aristocratic quality) could legitimately claim noble rank. In contrast, M. Jourdain, whilst clearly a man of substantial means, is still very close to his tradesman origins. Apart from the obvious ignorance of specific skills such as fencing and bowing, his money-lending practices and general *esprit marchand* stamp him with the attitude of the least prestigious sector of the bourgeoisie.

In theory it was not unrealistic for a man in M. Jourdain's position to acquire nobility. Even within the hierarchical structure of a *société d'états*, social mobility was made possible by wealth, and was actively encouraged by Louis XIV through a system of rewards. A conspicuous example of the socially ambitious *parvenu* was the Finance Minister Colbert. Nobility could be earned through service at Court or in the royal administration, or simply by buying a title from the King. Such procedures enabled talented or ambitious men to gain entry to the *noblesse d'office* or the *noblesse de lettres* respectively. These could be honourable conditions, albeit inferior in prestige to the old hereditary *noblesse d'épée*. A purchased title could certainly constitute a realistic aspiration for a man of M. Jourdain's extensive wealth. But to grasp the full incongruity of his ambitions, it is important to understand that the title of *gentilhomme* was unequivocally reserved for descendants of hereditary aristocrats. Furetière's entry under 'gentilhomme' reads: 'Homme noble d'extraction, qui ne doit point sa noblesse ni à sa charge, ni aux lettres du prince'. Richelet's *Dictionnaire Français* (1680) states that 'gentilhomme signifie qui est noble d'extraction, qui est noble de race et de naissance'. To contemporary eyes, M. Jourdain's ambition to become a *bourgeois gentilhomme* is literally and for ever impossible.

Molière's position in relation to the class structure of his age has been the subject of much debate. One tradition, which originated when Enlightenment *philosophes* sought to project their own ideological values on to his plays, sees him as hostile to the ruling aristocracy. The ascension of bourgeois values in the nineteenth century helped to consolidate the notion of Molière as the embodiment of middle-class *bon sens* (or mediocrity, according to one's point of view). A more recent thesis, argued by Bénichou and Cairncross, has replaced the bourgeois Molière by a Court artist identified with aristocratic values (*16*, *18*). For Bénichou, Molière was the scourge of the bourgeoisie. He writes, 'Il suffit de parcourir le théâtre de Molière pour se rendre compte que le bourgeois y est presque toujours médiocre et ridicule. Il n'est pas un seul des bourgeois de Molière qui présente, en tant que bourgeois, quelque élévation ou valeur morale' (*16*, pp.172-73). Still more recent socio-historical interpretations have aimed to show with greater precision how the behaviour and manners of his characters relate to the social reality of the time (*23*). Such approaches usually present Molière as an impartial observer of class differences. According to Gaines, the basic assumption of Molière's comedy is that each social condition has its own set of values expressed in an appropriate code of behaviour. Criticism is reserved for individuals who fail to observe the proper code for their social environment. In other words, relating the ideological perspective to the comic order, what is appropriate for one class will be comically inappropriate for another. Provincial dim-wits who behave as intellectuals, a servant who tries to ape a *bel esprit*, a *parvenu* who aspires to the status of hereditary nobility, are not objects of scorn because of the class they belong to but ridiculous because they deny their true station.

None of these approaches provides a wholly satisfactory explanation for Molière's treatment of class. Considered objectively, his comedies do not seem to reserve special criticism for any particular class as such. On the one hand, aristocratic characters, from Dom Juan or the petty *marquis* of *Le Misanthrope*, to Dorante in *Le Bourgeois gentilhomme*, invite disapproval or ridicule. On the other hand, middle-class characters represented by a whole range of *raisonneurs*, wives and young couples, are shown to be capable of sensible and even refined behaviour. And, contrary to Bénichou's thesis, certain middle-class values such as family and inheritance are positively validated by the plot structures on which the comedies often depend. Molière's monomaniacs typically express their obsession by damaging behaviour such as squandering the family wealth, disinheriting sons or marrying daughters to unsuitable partners. Such emphasis on domestic disruption only makes sense if one assumes that the order which is being disrupted is natural or desirable.

As an observer of human nature Molière interested himself in people of all conditions. It is presumably for this reason that his plays found favour with all theatre-going classes. Middle-class spectators were evidently able to laugh at the antics of an eccentric bourgeois without feeling threatened, just as the Court could laugh at aristocratic parasites, fops and bores. These facts hardly support the idea that Molière was engaged in partisan class propaganda. But Bénichou is basically correct when he identifies Molière with aristocratic values. The dominant perspective of *Le Bourgeois gentilhomme* is plainly that of the courtier, the person of discernment and taste. The ultimate value to which it appeals is the aristocratic one of *honnêteté*, which Cléonte possesses but M. Jourdain does not. The play takes for granted the natural superiority of aristocratic taste to middle-class vulgarity and confirms the unbridgeable gulf between them. On the question of money, for example, the play reflects an aristocratic outlook. For the true aristocrat, fastidiousness is reserved for food and dress, whilst money is treated with assumed disdain. This explains why M. Jourdain's scrupulous account-keeping is comic, whereas Dorante's cheating (which to modern spectators may seem reprehensible) is viewed with tolerant indulgence.

Within the predominantly courtly perspective, aristocratic values are not spared from gentle satire (see 46). If M. Jourdain is comically vulgar, the civilisation he envies is at times comically pedantic (the Maîtres) or comically over-precious (Cléonte in the *dépit amoureux*, Dorante's *galanterie*). The satire draws attention to an artificial civilisation, compared with which M. Jourdain's naïve unsophistication is not unattractive. Nevertheless, when M. Jourdain says wistfully 'Je ne vois rien de si beau que de hanter les grands seigneurs; il n'y a qu'honneur et que civilité avec eux', this cannot be dismissed as simply an eccentric personal attitude. It reflects an opinion which, at bottom, is assumed to be shared by Molière's audience. Affirming as it does the cultural hegemony of the aristocracy, it must have been very reassuring to Court spectators.

This is, apparently, a somewhat conformist attitude which can be disappointing to those who would like to see Molière as a subversive radical. Conformist it may be, but that is only to be expected if we remember that the role of the entertainer in the seventeenth century implied an uspoken contract under which the artist worked within the accepted rules of society. The notion of the artist as a lone outsider, alienated from society, is a post-Romantic ideal and anachronistic when applied to the seventeenth century. So, on most issues of the day such as religious belief, education for women, parental authority, Molière is generally found to have progressive but not revolutionary attitudes.

Reason and folly

There is a sense in which the play is truly subversive, but it is not an ideological subversion. Its true subversiveness lies in giving power to the imagination. Oddly enough, it is M. Jourdain, the most prosaic of men when judged by the standards of sophisticated society, who is the vehicle of poetic imagination. The comedy projects the inner world of an incorrigible dreamer, a *gentilhomme imaginaire*, and does so in defiance of all reason. Reason would require the *visionnaire* to be corrected. According to one perspective — that of the other characters, also shared at one level by the spectators — M. Jourdain only succeeds in making himself into a spectacle and a laughing-stock. But according to another perspective projected from within the *comédie-ballet*, the theatrical structure vindicates M. Jourdain's folly. Every significant stage of the action marks a further retreat of prosaic, everyday reality. Progressing from *bourgeois* to imaginary *gentilhomme* to Mamamouchi, the fantasist models the world according to his inner vision. Rather than forcing him into line with reason, the play brings the world into line with his folly. Prosaic judgement may find this contrary to morality but it is a logical and deeply satisfying outcome. Instead of the laughter of disapproval, it invites the liberating laughter that comes with recognition of the absurd.

In this respect *Le Bourgeois gentilhomme* marks the high point of Molière's aesthetic of unreason. The emphasis of his comic vision, as it evolved through the 1660s, can be seen to shift from the correction of abuses to a more tolerant indulgence of eccentricity. At the same time, a parallel development brought a movement from comic realism to a type of theatre which appeals more strongly to poetic fantasy. *Comédie-ballet*, where music and spectacle heighten the unreality, is the ideal medium for such an escapist aesthetic. In the process, Molière seems to have detached himself from the classical ideal of reason and aligned himself more with the outlook of the earlier humanist age exemplified by the Rabelais of *La Nef des fous* and the Erasmus of *The Praise of Folly*. Molière not only sees folly as an inescapable consequence of being human. He also suggests, like Erasmus, that if reason is necessary to moderate folly, folly is even more necessary to temper reason. In *Le Bourgeois gentilhomme* he renders folly attractive. Which of us, given the choice between M. Jourdain's blissful fiction with the joyous carnival atmosphere it creates, and the prosaic reality represented by Mme Jourdain's common sense, would not prefer the former?

I am not suggesting that M. Jourdain is clinically mad. The point is that in the carnivalesque world of *comédie-ballet* Molière unleashes in their purest form the irrational tendencies that are within each of us. In an earlier *comédie-ballet*, *M. de Pourceaugnac* (1669), he wrote:

> Lorsque pour rire on s'assemble
> Les plus sages, ce me semble,
> Sont ceux qui sont les plus fous. (III, 10)

In the same way, in *Le Bourgeois gentilhomme*, he presents us with the paradox of M. Jourdain triumphantly exclaiming, at the very moment when the world falls in with his madness: 'Ah! voilà tout le monde raisonnable'. Covielle may proclaim his own sanity — 'tout ceci n'est fait que pour nous ajuster aux visions de votre mari' — but the world is nevertheless playing the role assigned to it by the madman. At this point the permitted fantasy of the Court entertainer resembles the licensed madness of the jester whose antics expose the fundamental folly of the world. The topsy-turvy world it reveals to us echoes the words of Erasmus:

> Without folly, the world cannot exist for a moment. For
> is not all that is done among mortals full of folly; is it
> not performed by fools and for fools?

This seems to me to be the play's ultimate lesson.

    Bienséance demands that M. Jourdain's unruly folly be re-absorbed in a courtly perspective. As the anarchic vision dissolves into the final ballet, harmony, good taste and sense reign once more, guaranteed by the wisdom of the King who presides over the spectacle. Reason finally prevails over unreason. But we now know that it is an illusory triumph of the artificial over human nature.

Bibliography

A. EDITIONS OF THE PLAY

1. Molière, *Œuvres*, ed. E. Despois & P. Mesnard, Paris: Hachette, 1873-1900, 13 vols (vol.8).
2. *Le Bourgeois gentilhomme*, ed. H. Gaston Hall, University of London Press, 1966. The best modern edition. Now regrettably out of print, it is worth consulting for a scrupulous edition based on the text of the 1671 edition, and for its illuminating analysis of the play.
3. *Le Bourgeois gentilhomme*, ed. Yves Hucher, Classiques Larousse, 1970. Now replaced by:-
3a. *Le Bourgeois gentilhomme*, ed. Bernard Pluchart-Simon, Classiques Larousse, 1990. Accessible and inexpensive.
4. *Le Bourgeois gentilhomme*, ed. Jacques Morel, Livre de Poche, 1985. Takes account of more recent critical ideas about the play.
5. *Le Bourgeois gentilhomme*, ed. R.A. Wilson, Nelson (Harrap's French Classics), 1954. Dated.

B. BACKGROUND STUDIES

6. Adam, Antoine, *Histoire de la littérature française au XVIIe siècle*, Paris: Domat, 1953, 5 vols (vol. 3).
7. Arvieux, Laurent d', *Mémoires du Chevalier d'Arvieux*, Paris: Delespine, 1735, 6 vols (vol. 4).
8. Bergson, Henri, *Le Rire. Essai sur la signification du comique*, Paris: Presses Universitaires de France, 1940 (first published 1900).
9. Christout, M.F., *Le Ballet de cour de Louis XIV*, Paris: Picard, Collection 'Mises en scène', 1967.
10. Lancaster, H.C., *A History of French Dramatic Literature in the Seventeenth Century*, Baltimore/London, Johns Hopkins University Press, 1929-42, 10 vols (Part III: *The period of Molière*).
11. Lintilhac, Eugène, *Histoire du théâtre en France*, Paris: Flammarion, 1904-11, 5 vols (vol. 2).

12. Lough, John, *French Theatre Audiences in the Seventeenth and Eighteenth Centuries*, Oxford U.P., 1957.
13. Martino, Pierre, *L'Orient dans la littérature française au 17e et au 18e siècle*, Paris: Hachette, 1906.
14. Pernoud, Régine, *Histoire de la bourgeoisie en France*, 2 vols, Paris: Seuil, 1960-62.
15. Pure, Abbé de, *L'Idée des spectacles anciens et modernes*, Paris, 1668.

C. STUDIES OF MOLIERE

16. Bénichou, Paul, *Morales du grand siècle*, Paris: Gallimard, 1948.
17. Bray, René, *Molière, homme de théâtre*, Paris: Mercure de France, 1954.
18. Cairncross, John, *Molière bourgeois et libertin*, Paris: Nizet, 1963.
19. Defaux, Gérard, *Molière ou les métamorphoses du comique*, Lexington, Ky: French Forum, 1980.
20. Descotes, Maurice, *Les Grands Rôles du théâtre de Molière*, Paris: Presses Universitaires de France, 1960.
21. Donneau de Visé, Jean (and others), *Molière jugé par ses contemporains*, ed. A. Poulet-Malassis, Paris, 1877.
22. Fernandez, Ramon, *La Vie de Molière*, Paris: Gallimard, 1929.
23. Gaines, James F., *Social structures in Molière's theatre*, Ohio State U.P., 1984.
24. Grimarest, *Vie de Monsieur de Molière* (1705), repr. Paris: Renaissance du livre, 1930.
25. Guicharnaud, J., *Molière, une aventure théâtrale*, Paris: Gallimard, 1963.
26. Howarth, W.D., *Molière, a playwright and his audience*, Cambridge U.P., 1982.
27. Hubert, J.D., *Molière and the comedy of intellect*, California U.P., 1962.
28. Larroumet, Gustave, *La Comédie de Molière: l'auteur et le milieu*, Paris: Hachette, 1887.
29. Michaut, Gustave, *Les Luttes de Molière*, Paris: Hachette, 1925.
30. Moore, W.G., *Molière, a new criticism*, Oxford: Clarendon Press, 1949.
31. Sainte-Beuve, *Portraits littéraires*, Paris: Garnier, 1862, 3 vols (vol. 2).
32. Simon, Alfred, *Molière, une vie*, Lyon: La Manufacture, 1987.

D. ON COMÉDIE-BALLET AND LE BOURGEOIS GENTILHOMME

33. Abraham, Claude, *On the structure of Molière's comédie-ballets*, Paris: Papers on French Seventeenth Century Literature/Biblio 17, 1984.

34. Chevalley, Sylvie, ed., *Le Bourgeois gentilhomme*, Paris: Comédie-Française, 1969.

35. ——, ed., *Le Bourgeois gentilhomme* ('Les Dossiers Molière'), Geneva: Minkoff, 1975.

36. Copeau, Jacques, 'Les comédie-ballets', in *Registres*, II, Paris: Gallimard, 1976.

37. Defaux, Gérard, 'Rêve et réalité dans *Le Bourgeois Gentilhomme*', *Dix-septième siècle*, 117 (1977), pp.19-33.

38. Garapon, Robert, 'La langue et le style des différents personnages du *Bourgeois Gentilhomme*', *Le Français Moderne*, XXVI, 2 (1958), pp.103-12.

39. Martino, Pierre, 'La cérémonie turque du *Bourgeois Gentilhomme*', *Revue d'Histoire Littéraire*, 18 (1911), pp.36-60.

40. Marion, Jean, 'Molière a-t-il songé à Colbert en composant le personnage de M. Jourdain?', *Revue d'Histoire Littéraire de la France*, XLV (1938), 145-80.

41. Maurice-Amour, Lila, 'Rythme dans les comédies-ballets de Molière', *Revue d'Histoire du Théâtre*, 26 (1974), pp.118-31.

42. Maxfield-Miller, Elizabeth, 'The real M. Jourdain of the *Bourgeois Gentilhomme*', *Studies in Philology* , 56 (1959), pp.62-73.

43. Mazouer, Charles, '*Le Mariage forcé* de Molière, Lully et Beauchamp: esthétique de la comédie-ballet', in *Dramaturgies, langages dramatiques*, Paris: Nizet, 1986.

44. Mélèse, Pierre, 'Molière à la Cour', *Dix-septième siècle*, no. 98-99 (1973), pp.57-66.

45. Mongrédien, Georges, 'Molière et Lulli', *Dix-septième siècle*, no. 98-99 (1973), pp.3-16.

46. Mourgues, O. de, '*Le Bourgeois gentilhomme* as a criticism of civilisation', in Howarth & Thomas (eds), *Molière stage and study*, Oxford: Clarendon, 1973, pp.170-84.

47. Pellisson, Maurice, *Les Comédies-ballets de Molière*, Paris: Hachette, 1914.

48. Shaw, David, '*Le Bourgeois gentilhomme* and the seventeenth century social revolution', *Modern Languages*, LX, 4 (December 1979), pp.211-18.

49. Talamon, René, 'La Marquise du *Bourgeois Gentilhomme*', *Modern Language Notes*, 50 (1935), pp.369-75.

ADDENDUM

The following study appeared while this book was in the press:-
Hall, H. Gaston, *Molière's* Le Bourgeois gentilhomme: *context and stagecraft*, 'Durham Modern Languages Series', Univ. of Durham, 1990.

CRITICAL GUIDES TO FRENCH TEXTS

edited by

Roger Little, Wolfgang van Emden, David Williams

1. **David Bellos.** Balzac: La Cousine Bette.
2. **Rosemarie Jones.** Camus: L'Etranger *and* La Chute.
3. **W.D Redfern.** Queneau: Zazie dans le métro.
4. **R.C. Knight.** Corneille: Horace.
5. **Christopher Todd.** Voltaire: Dictionnaire philosophique.
6. **J.P. Little.** Beckett: En attendant Godot *and* Fin de partie.
7. **Donald Adamson.** Balzac: Illusions perdues.
8. **David Coward.** Duras: Moderato cantabile.
9. **Michael Tilby.** Gide: Les Faux-Monnayeurs.
10. **Vivienne Mylne.** Diderot: La Religieuse.
11. **Elizabeth Fallaize.** Malraux: La Voie Royale.
12. **H.T Barnwell.** Molière: Le Malade imaginaire.
13. **Graham E. Rodmell.** Marivaux: Le Jeu de l'amour et du hasard *and* Les Fausses Confidences.
14. **Keith Wren.** Hugo: Hernani *and* Ruy Blas.
15. **Peter S. Noble.** Beroul's Tristan *and the* Folie de Berne.
16. **Paula Clifford.** Marie de France: Lais.
17. **David Coward.** Marivaux: La Vie de Marianne *and* Le Paysan parvenu.
18. **J.H. Broome.** Molière: L'Ecole des femmes *and* Le Misanthrope.
19. **B.G. Garnham.** Robbe-Grillet: Les Gommes *and* Le Voyeur.
20. **J.P. Short.** Racine: Phèdre.
21. **Robert Niklaus.** Beaumarchais: Le Mariage de Figaro.
22. **Anthony Cheal Pugh.** Simon: Histoire.
23. **Lucie Polak.** Chrétien de Troyes: Cligés.
24. **John Cruickshank.** Pascal: Pensées.
25. **Ceri Crossley.** Musset: Lorenzaccio.
26. **J.W Scott.** Madame de Lafayette: La Princesse de Clèves.
27. **John Holyoake.** Montaigne: Essais.
28. **Peter Jimack.** Rousseau: Emile.
29. **Roger Little.** Rimbaud: Illuminations.

30. **Barbara Wright and David Scott.** Baudelaire: La Fanfarlo *and* Le Spleen de Paris.
31. **Haydn Mason.** Cyrano de Bergerac: L'Autre Monde.
32. **Glyn S. Burgess.** Chrétien de Troyes: Erec et Enide.
33. **S. Beynon John.** Anouilh: L'Alouette *and* Pauvre Bitos.
34. **Robin Buss.** Vigny: Chatterton.
35. **David Williams.** Rousseau: Les Rêveries du promeneur solitaire.
36. **Ronnie Butler.** Zola: La Terre.
37. **John Fox.** Villon: Poems.
38. **C.E.J. Dolamore.** Ionesco: Rhinocéros.
39. **Robert Lethbridge.** Maupassant: Pierre et Jean.
40. **David Curtis.** Descartes: Discours de la Méthode.
41. **Peter Cogman.** Hugo: Les Contemplations.
42. **Rosemary Lloyd.** Mallarmé: Poésies.
43. **M. Adereth.** Aragon: The Resistance Poems.
44. **Keith Wren.** Vigny: Les Destinées.
45. **Kathleen M. Hall and Margaret B. Wells.** Du Bellay: Poems.
46. **Geoffrey Bremner.** Diderot: Jacques le fataliste.
47. **Peter Dunwoodie.** Camus: L'Envers et l'Endroit *and* L'Exil et le Royaume.
48. **Michael Sheringham.** Beckett: Molloy.
49. **J.F. Falvey.** Diderot: Le Neveu de Rameau.
50. **Dennis Fletcher.** Voltaire: Lettres philosophiques.
51. **Philip Robinson.** Bernardin de Saint-Pierre: Paul et Virginie.
52. **Richard Griffiths.** Garnier: Les Juifves.
53. **Paula Clifford.** La Chastelaine de Vergi *and* Jean Renart: Le Lai de l'ombre.
54. **Robin Buss.** Cocteau: Les Enfants terribles.
55. **Tony Hunt.** Chrétien de Troyes: Yvain.
56. **Robert Gibson.** Alain-Fournier: Le Grand Meaulnes.
57. **James J. Supple.** Racine: Bérénice.
58. **Timothy Unwin.** Constant: Adolphe.
59. **David Shaw.** Molière: Les Précieuses ridicules.
60. **Roger Cardinal.** Breton: Nadja.

61. **Geoffrey N. Bromiley.** Thomas's Tristan *and the* Folie Tristan d'Oxford.
62. **R.J. Howells.** Rousseau: Julie ou la Nouvelle Héloïse.
63. **George Evans.** Lesage: Crispin rival de son maître *and* Turcaret.
64. **Paul Reed.** Sartre: La Nausée.
65. **Roger Mclure.** Sarraute: Le Planétarium.
66. **Denis Boak.** Sartre: Les Mots.
67. **Pamela M. Moores.** Vallès: L'Enfant.
68. **Simon Davies.** Laclos: Les Liaisons dangereuses.
69. **Keith Beaumont.** Jarry: Ubu Roi.
70. **G.J. Mallinson.** Molière: L'Avare.
71. **Susan Taylor-Horrex.** Verlaine: Fêtes galantes *and* Romances sans paroles.
72. **Malcolm Cook.** Lesage: Gil Blas.
73. **Sheila Bell.** Sarraute: Portrait d'un inconnu *and* Vous les entendez?
74. **W.D. Howarth.** Corneille: Le Cid.
75. **Peter Jimack.** Diderot: Supplément au Voyage de Bougainville.
76. **Christopher Lloyd.** Maupassant: Bel-Ami.
77. **David H. Walker.** Gide: Les Nourritures terrestres *and* La Symphonie pastorale
78. **Noël Peacock.** Molière: Les Femmes savantes.
79. **Jean H. Duffy.** Butor: La Modification.
80. **J.P. Little.** Genet: Les Nègres.
81. **John Campbell.** Racine: Britannicus.
82. **Malcolm Quainton.** D'Aubigné: Les Tragiques.
83. **Henry Phillips.** Racine: Mithridate.
84. **S. Beynon John.** Saint-Exupéry: Vol de Nuit *and* Terre des hommes.
85. **John Trethewey.** Corneille: L'Illusion comique *and* Le Menteur.
86. **John Dunkley.** Beaumarchais: Le Barbier de Séville.
87. **Valerie Minogue.** Zola: L'Assommoir.
88. **Kathleen Hall.** Rabelais: Pantagruel and Gargantua.